# My Body,
# My Self
## for Girls

## Other books by Lynda Madaras

*My Feelings, My Self:*
*A Growing-Up Guide for Girls*
with Area Madaras

*"The What's Happening to My Body?"*
*Book for Girls*
with Area Madaras

*"The What's Happening to My Body?"*
*Book for Boys*
with Area Madaras

*Lynda Madaras Talks to Teens*
*About AIDS: An Essential Guide for*
*Parents, Teachers and Young People*

*Womancare: A Gynecological Guide*
*to Your Body*
with Jane Patterson, M.D.

*Woman Doctor: The Education of*
*Jane Patterson, M.D.*
with Jane Patterson, M.D.

*Great Expectations* with Leigh Adams

*The Alphabet Connection*
with Pam Palewicz-Rousseau

*Child's Play*

# My Body, My Self for Girls

## The "What's Happening to My Body" Workbook

**Lynda Madaras and Area Madaras**

**Newmarket Press**
*New York*

We'd like to thank three women who helped us put together this book—
*Doe Coover,*
the world's greatest literary agent,
*Eartha Sewell,*
a wonderful sexuality educator,
*and Jill Ganon,*
a terrific writer.

And, we'd like to dedicate this book
to them and their children—
*Molly, Tom, Seth, and Miles.*

Quantity Purchases:

Companies, professional groups, clubs, and other organizations may qualify for special terms when ordering quantities of this title. For information, write Special Sales, Newmarket Press, 18 East 48th Street, New York, N.Y. 10017; call (212) 832-3575; fax (212) 832-3629; or email sales@newmarketpress.com.
www.newmarketpress.com

**Library of Congress Cataloging-in-Publication Data**

Madaras, Lynda
   My body, my self for girls:  the "what's happening to my body?" workbook/
Lynda Madaras and Area Madaras.
         p.          cm.
         ISBN 1-55704-441-4
   1. Teenage girls—Growth—Juvenile literature.  2. Teenage girls—Physiology—Juvenile literature.
   3. Puberty—Juvenile literature.  4. Sex instruction for girls—Juvenile literature.
I. Madaras, Area.   II. Title.
RJ144.M29   1993
612.6'61'08352—dc20                               93-19189
                                    CIP

*Book design by Deborah Daly*
*Drawings by Susan Spellman and Lisa Hale*
MANUFACTURED IN THE UNITED STATES OF AMERICA

# Contents

# Preface

Hi, I'm Lynda Madaras and I'm Area Madaras.

e're the mother and daughter team who put this book together (with a lot of help from our friends).

Some years ago, we wrote another book called *The What's Happening To My Body? Book For Girls* that explained the physical and emotional changes a girl goes through during her preteen and teen years, as her body changes from a child's to a woman's body. This time of changing is known as puberty, and the book explained how and why puberty happens and answered the many questions that had come up in Lynda's sex education classes over the years.

This book is a companion to our first book, though you don't need *The What's Happening To My Body? Book* to use this one. This book covers many of the same topics covered in our earlier book, though not in as much detail. The big difference between the two books is that this is a workbook, with exercises, quizzes and other activities that will help you learn about the changes that take place in your body during puberty.

Like our first book, this book owes a great deal to the many girls and boys who have been students in Lynda's classes at Sequoyah School over the years and to the families who have attended our puberty and sexuality workshops. Much of the material in this book was developed and refined with their help. Indeed, without their kind patience when exercises and activities didn't work out as planned and their enthusiasm when they did, this book would not have been written.

We hope that you (and the friends and family members you'll recruit for some of the activities) enjoy the activities and exercises in the book and that it will answer some of the questions you'll have as you enter this new stage of your life.

Lynda Madaras
Area Madaras,
July 2000

# PART ONE

# WHAT'S HAPPENING TO YOU?

**You're going through puberty!** During the pre-teen and teen years, girls go through a series of physical and emotional changes as their bodies develop from children's bodies into women's bodies. This time of changing is called puberty.

This book is about you and the changes that take place in your body during your puberty years. It explains how, when, and why puberty happens and is filled with quizzes, exercises, and other activities for you to do. Throughout the book, you'll be asked to record your thoughts and feelings and to write about what's happening to you. In fact, before you're through, this book will not only be *about* you, it will be *by* you as well!

We hope that you'll have fun with the book, that you'll learn a thing or two, and that you'll come back to it from time to time as you move through puberty. We hope, too, that you'll hang on to the book, and that if you one day have a daughter or another special young woman in your life, you'll give her this special puberty book written by and about you!

**P.S.** If this book is yours, you're free to write in it, doodle on it, or scribble all over it. But if it's a library book, you'll need to do the exercises and writing on separate sheets of paper or in a notebook.

# You

ince this book is all about you, let's start with you:

I am _____ years and _____ months old.

I am _____ feet and _____ inches tall.

I weigh _____ pounds.

I go to school at _____.

I am in the _____ grade.

I live with _____.

When I'm alone I like to _____

_____.

When I'm with my friends we like to _____

_____.

My best friend and I talk about _____

_____.

An adult I can really talk to is _____

_____.

One thing I really like about myself is _____

_____.

# PUBERTY CHANGES

✿ Growth spurt causes rapid increase in height—you grow taller at a faster rate than ever before.

✿ Oil glands in scalp become more active—your hair may be oily, and you may need to wash it more often.

✿ Nipples and surrounding skin get darker in color.

✿ Breasts enlarge—they may be tender or sore.

✿ Hips broaden—your waist seems smaller in comparison.

✿ Curly pubic hairs grow on the vulva (the area between your legs).*

✿ Hair on legs also may increase and may be darker in color.

✿ Growth spurt affects feet first, causing rapid growth. You may find that you outgrow your shoes before they're hardly worn.

✿ Skin produces more oils— you may develop pimples.

✿ Hair grows under arms.

✿ Underarm perspiration (sweat) glands are more active—you develop an adult body odor.

✿ Hair on arms may increase and may be darker in color.

✿ During puberty, you may notice an increase in vaginal discharge, and you will also have your first menstrual period. To find out more about these changes, turn to the next page.

---

*Many people call this area of the body "the vagina," but as you'll learn in Part 5, the vagina is actually up inside the body. The proper name for this part of the female body is the vulva.

# Vaginal Discharge

*I have noticed a clear and also a milky white discharge from my vagina. Could you tell me what this means? I'm wondering if this is normal.*

During puberty, you may start to have a small amount of a clear milky white fluid, or discharge, from the walls of the vagina that may leave a slight yellowish stain on your underpants as it dries. This fluid is called vaginal discharge, and it is completely normal, another sign that your body is maturing.

Vaginal discharge helps to keep your vagina clean and healthy. As we'll explain in Part 5, the discharge is made up of fluids and cells shed from the walls of the vagina. Just as the skin on the surface of our bodies is constantly shedding old cells, the skin of the vagina also sheds cells. The body makes fluids to wash away these cells and cleanse the vagina. As you go through puberty, the shedding of old cells from the vaginal walls speeds up. More fluid is made, and a girl may notice more discharge from her vaginal opening.

Many girls first notice this discharge a year or two before their first menstrual periods. Others don't notice it until after they've started menstruating, and some never have much discharge at all. Those who do notice the discharge may find that there's more discharge on some days than others and that the color and consistency of the discharge changes at certain times. You'll learn more about this in Part 5, but for now let's talk about what many girls consider the biggest, most dramatic puberty change—the Big M, menstruation.

# Menstruation

*My mom told me about menstruating. I am excited, but scared too. We learned about menstrual periods at school, too. But could you tell me exactly when mine will come?*

During puberty, girls also begin menstruating. When a girl menstruates, a bloody (but harmless) fluid called the menstrual flow dribbles out of the vaginal opening. The menstrual flow lasts for a period of two to seven days. Grown women usually have a menstrual period about once a month. But as you'll learn in Part 5, girls who have just begun menstruating may have their periods more or less often than this.

No one can say exactly when a girl will have her first menstrual period, but in Part 6, we'll be giving you some clues that will help you make an educated guess as to when you can expect to begin menstruating.

Hearing about menstruation and the other puberty changes all at once can be scary and a bit overwhelming, but these changes don't happen overnight. Puberty happens slowly and gradually, over a period of months and years, so you'll have plenty of time to get used to these changes. And, remember, billions of human beings have managed to make it through puberty. You will too!

You may have already noticed some puberty changes in your body. In fact, you may be so far along that your body practically looks like an adult woman's. Or you may not have noticed many (or any) of these changes yet. Since this book is about you, let's see where you are. Get out your pencil and take a look at the puberty checklist on the next page.

# Check It Out

I have noticed the following changes in my body (check all the ones that apply):

☐ My feet seem to be growing very fast.

☐ I have begun to grow taller at a faster rate than ever before.

☐ There are curly pubic hairs growing on my vulva.

☐ My breasts have started to develop.

☐ The skin around my nipples is getting darker in color.

☐ I perspire (sweat) more.

☐ My body's odor has begun to change.

☐ I have noticed vaginal discharge on my underpants.

☐ There is more hair on my arms and legs and/or it is darker in color.

☐ My skin and hair are more oily.

☐ I have more pimples.

☐ My hips are getting wider and my body shape is changing.

☐ Hair is growing under my arms (in the armpits).

☐ I have begun to menstruate.

# Can You Guess How Old These Girls Are?

Anna is ＿＿＿ years old.     Katie is ＿＿＿ years old.     Jessie is ＿＿＿ years old.

**Answer:** They're all the same age—twelve years old.

As you can see, girls of the same age are often at different stages of development. We each have our own personal timetable of growth and development. Some of us develop early, others a little later. Some girls begin to grow pubic hair and develop breasts while they're still in grade school. For others, these changes don't happen until their teen years. For most girls, though, these changes happen between the ages of nine and eleven.

Remember, though, you may not be like most girls. Being different—starting to develop earlier or later—than the other girls your age isn't always easy. Maybe it will help you to remember:

● You're normal! You may be developing at a different time, but you're still perfectly normal.

● You won't be ahead—or behind—forever. The other girls will soon catch up to you, or you'll catch up to them.

● No matter where you are in your development, you're unique, one of a kind. In the whole universe, there's not another one like you. Feel special!

# STAGES OF THE FEMALE LIFECYCLE

hen you think in terms of your whole life, being fast or slow to develop really doesn't matter much at all. After all, we all end up in the same place—grown up! (And then you'll wonder what all the fuss was about!)

The illustration below explains the stages of the female life cycle (of which puberty is only one).

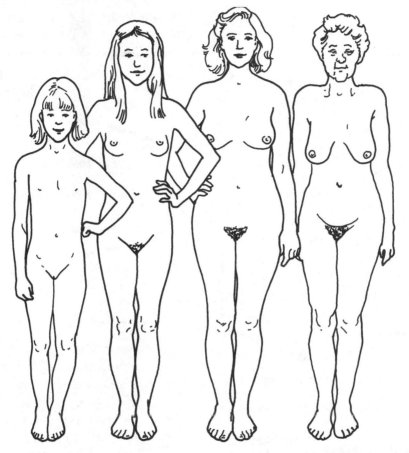

**CHILDHOOD:** This stage begins at birth and continues until puberty begins.

**PUBERTY:** The transition stage between childhood and adulthood, when a girl's body matures and she begins menstruating.

**REPRODUCTIVE YEARS:** During this mature, or adult, stage, a woman is capable of reproducing (of having a baby).

**MENOPAUSE:** Menopause begins when a woman stops having her monthly menstrual periods and is no longer capable of having a baby.

# Thoughts & Feelings: GROWING UP

I was really jazzed about it. Then, two seconds later, I had this really scary feeling—"Oh, no, I'm not ready for this."

—Nygie, age 11

It's a "Hey, whoopie, I'm finally growing up!" kind of feeling.

—Nadine, age 13

I didn't start developing until I was seventeen. I thought there was something horribly wrong, like maybe I was really a man instead of a woman.

—Vanessa, age 21

I'm not sure I'm exactly looking forward to all these things ... Puberty is beginning to sound like some kind of disease.

—Jennie, age 11

I started developing, and no one else was. I used to wrap one of those bandages, the kind you put on a sprained ankle, around my chest to make me flat. I kept my coat on as much as I could and wore baggy clothes all the time. Now that I'm older, I can laugh about it, but back then it wasn't funny at all.

—Angela, age 22

I started developing when I was eleven... I was glad, but I was embarrassed, especially at school.

—Jill, age 15

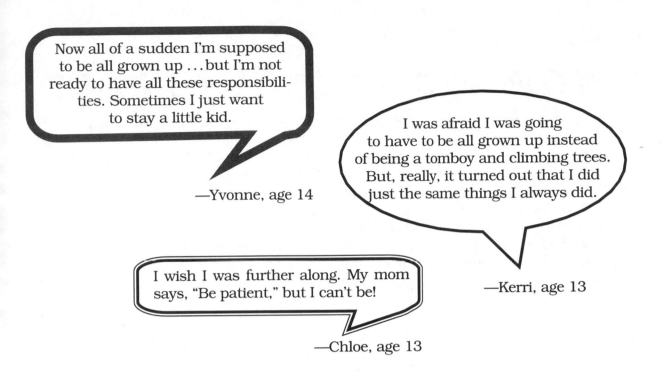

Now all of a sudden I'm supposed to be all grown up ... but I'm not ready to have all these responsibilities. Sometimes I just want to stay a little kid.

—Yvonne, age 14

I was afraid I was going to have to be all grown up instead of being a tomboy and climbing trees. But, really, it turned out that I did just the same things I always did.

—Kerri, age 13

I wish I was further along. My mom says, "Be patient," but I can't be!

—Chloe, age 13

# WHAT ABOUT YOU?

You've heard what these girls and women have to say, now it's your turn. On the next page, you'll find a freewriting exercise with space for you to write your own thoughts and feelings.

## Freewriting (How To)

Just write whatever comes into your head. It doesn't necessarily have to make sense, and you don't have to worry about spelling and punctuation. (It's called freewriting because it's free of the usual rules about writing.) There is, however, one rule: Once you've started writing, don't stop until you reach the end of the page.

If you get stuck, don't know how you feel, can't think of anything to say, write just that—"I'm stuck," or "I can't think of anything to say." Write it over and over if you have to, just so long as you keep writing, without stopping until you've filled all the blank space.

# HOW DO YOU FEEL?

What are your feelings about growing up and the way your body is—or soon will be—changing? Are you excited, scared, or both? How far along are you? Do you wish you were further along? How do you feel about the changes you've noticed so far? Are you excited about the changes to come or would you rather just forget the whole thing? If you're already well into puberty, do you remember what you felt like before? Do you feel different now? What questions do you still have? What are you feeling right now?

Use the space below to freewrite your thoughts and feelings about puberty, your changing body, and growing up.

# Why It Happens

We've told you a bit about what happens during puberty, now let's talk about why it happens.

Menstruation and the other changes that take place during puberty happen because your body is getting ready for a time in your life when you may decide to have a baby. Of course, the fact that you're physically capable of reproduction (having a baby) doesn't mean that you are ready to be a parent. But during puberty, the body is preparing itself for a time when you may decide to start a family.

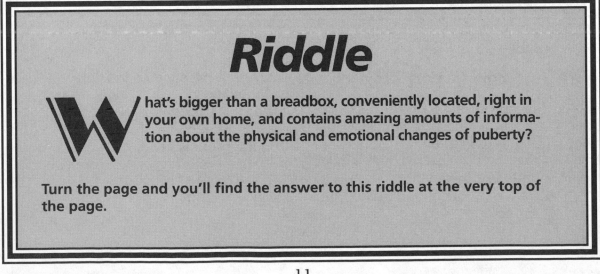

# ASKING QUESTIONS...FINDING ANSWERS

If you're like most girls, you probably have a lot of questions about puberty changes and this whole business of how babies are made. We hope this book will answer some of these questions and help you learn the facts in a way that's fun and entertaining.

But we won't pretend that this book will answer all of your questions. For one thing, it's a workbook/journal/exercise book more than an information/facts book. We've written an information/facts book about puberty and it's listed, along with similar books, in the resource section (see page 118).

But no book, no matter how good, can answer all of your questions. Fortunately, there is a solution close at hand. To find out what it is, solve the riddle in the box below.

---

# Riddle

What's bigger than a breadbox, conveniently located, right in your own home, and contains amazing amounts of information about the physical and emotional changes of puberty?

Turn the page and you'll find the answer to this riddle at the very top of the page.

# THE ANSWER:
## Your Mom, Your Dad or Whatever Adult(s) You Live With

These folks are the answer. They're the most logical ones to turn to when you have questions, need advice, or just want to talk about what's happening to you. They can understand what you're going through—after all, they've been through it too!

What if you're ready and willing, but your parents are too chicken to talk?

Or, maybe you're the one who's all red in the face—too shy and embarrassed to talk.

If you've had these sorts of problems, you're not alone. Take a look at the next page.

## Easier Said Than Done?

As the girls quoted on the opposite page point out, talking to your parents about puberty isn't always the easiest thing in the world. Does what they have to say sound familiar to you?

If you have problems talking to your parents (or even if you don't), try the exercises on the next few pages. They'll help you bring up the subject and help your parents remember what it was like to go through puberty. They'll also help you get past the embarrassment that so often keeps parents and kids from talking about these things.

My dad's a doctor, but I feel very uncomfortable asking him questions about growing up.
—Melinda, age 12

My mom and I have always talked freely about puberty and sex, but some things I still don't talk to her about. —Anne, age 13

I feel very uncomfortable because I'm afraid to ask them a question like, "Why don't I have my period yet, when I'm thirteen and a half?" I'm afraid they'll have this really weird look on their faces....I have a sister that is older...but if I ask her that question she'll just smile and say, "Why don't you ask Mom and Dad?" And I'll say because I'm afraid.
—Jessie, age 13 1/2

My mother died when I was six and I never knew my father. I don't feel comfortable talking to my grandmother, she thinks you shouldn't have a crush until you're sixteen or something.
—Michelle, age 11

My friends' mothers talk to them about bras and periods, but my mother never talks to me. —Brenda, age 10

In fifth grade we had sex ed— boys in one room, girls in another. But it was about as informative as a blank book. When I came home I asked my mom. She didn't know much either. (Her mother had treated it as a curse.) —Robin, age 12

I ask my mom and she tells me to go ask my dad. He says, "Go ask your mom."
Sharon, age 9

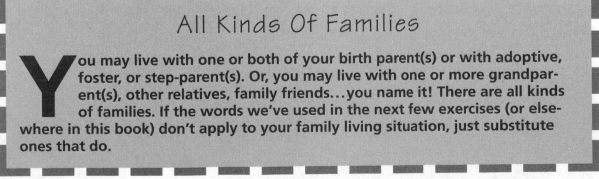

## All Kinds Of Families

**Y**ou may live with one or both of your birth parent(s) or with adoptive, foster, or step-parent(s). Or, you may live with one or more grandparent(s), other relatives, family friends...you name it! There are all kinds of families. If the words we've used in the next few exercises (or elsewhere in this book) don't apply to your family living situation, just substitute ones that do.

# Remember When...

Explain to your parent(s) that you need their help with one of your workbook exercises. Then have them answer the questions below.

## INTERVIEW I: *When you were my age...*

What was your favorite radio or TV show?_____

What kind of music did you listen to? _____

Who was your best friend?_____

What did you most enjoy doing? _____

What did you want to be when you grew up?_____

Where did you go to school? _____

Did they teach puberty or sex education in your school?_____

Did your parents talk to you about puberty and how babies are made?_____

Do you wish they'd talked to you more?_____


## INTERVIEW II: *When you were going through puberty...*

Did you start to develop earlier, later, or about the same time as your friends?_____

What were the first changes you noticed and how old were you? _____

_____

_____

How did you feel about these changes? _____

_____

What did your parents tell you about puberty and how babies are made? _____

_____

_____

menstruation PUBIC HAIR

buying a bra

using tampons VAGINAL DISCHARGE

crushes

MAKING DECISIONS ABOUT SEX

dating perspiration

using a deodorant

how babies are made

## Talking About Puberty

In the conversation balloon above, we've listed some of the topics that parents and daughters might talk about during the puberty years. Can you think of any others?

**Part I:** For the first part of the exercise, you and a parent will take turns filling in the empty balloon below. You go

first. Write a "puberty topic" that parents and daughters might want to discuss in the balloon. Then, pass the book to your parent and have him/her write one. Continue taking turns until you've either filled up the entire space (in which case you're both winners) or until one of you can't think of another topic (in which case the last person to make an entry is the winner). When you've finished, go on to the next page.

15

**Part II:** Look at the two conversation balloons on page 15 and pick the three topics that would be most embarrassing or hardest for you to discuss with your parent. Write the three topics in the spaces below.

Then, cover up your answers and have your parent list the three topics that she/he would find most embarrassing or hardest to discuss with you.

1) _____

2) _____

3) _____

1) _____

2) _____

3) _____

● ● ● ● ● ● ● ● ● ● ● ● ● ● ● ● ● ● ● ● ● ● ● ● ● ● ● ● ● ● ● ● ● ● ● ● ● ● ● ●

**Part III:** Now compare your lists, answering the questions and following the instructions below.

Do the same or similar topics appear on both of your lists? Put a check mark in front of any items that appear on both lists.

Other than items which are the same on both lists, are there topics on the other person's list that you too would find difficult or embarrassing to discuss? If so, mark those items with check marks too.

Are there any topics on your lists that are so embarrassing for you that it would be very difficult or impossible to discuss the topic? Put a check mark in front of these topics as well.

Almost all parents and daughters have at least some degree of embarrassment about one topic or another, and this can make it difficult to talk about these things. But by doing this exercise, you should have a clearer idea of just where you may run into difficulties. You may even find simply doing this exercise and

identifying the embarrassment have already made it easier to talk about these things!

Below are some other suggestions you may find useful. Read and discuss each suggestion, putting an ✗ in front of those that might work for you.

❑ Have a third person (a doctor, nurse, or counselor) talk with both of you about the topic.

❑ Read books or pamphlets, watch videos about the topic together, and talk about it (see Resources, page 118).

❑ Have the parent read a book or talk to another person and then share the information with the daughter.

❑ Find another person (family member, nurse, or doctor) to talk to the daughter.

# Part Two

# ON YOUR MARK, GET SET, GROW!

**Y**ou may have noticed that your feet are getting bigger or that you are growing taller faster than ever before. This is called the puberty growth spurt. It is a period of especially rapid growth. It is one of the early changes that happen when a girl goes through puberty. During the growth spurt, our bones start growing faster, our feet get bigger, and we get taller.

The growth spurt affects the bones throughout our bodies—some bones more than others, though. As a result, the proportions of our bodies (the size of certain parts of the body in comparison to others) also change as we mature. Even our facial bones are affected, and we may look quite different from when we were just little kids.

In addition to a spurt in height, there's also a rapid increase in weight during puberty. In fact, it's not unusual for a girl to put on fifteen pounds in a single year. Fat pads grow on our hips and thighs, and there's an increase in the overall fat content of our bodies. Thus, we begin to develop a more rounded, womanly figure.

The way we look changes a good deal during puberty. We hope that the information, exercises, and activities in this section will help you understand your changing size and shape and adjust to your new "looks."

# GROWING UP ...
# AND UP ... AND UP ...

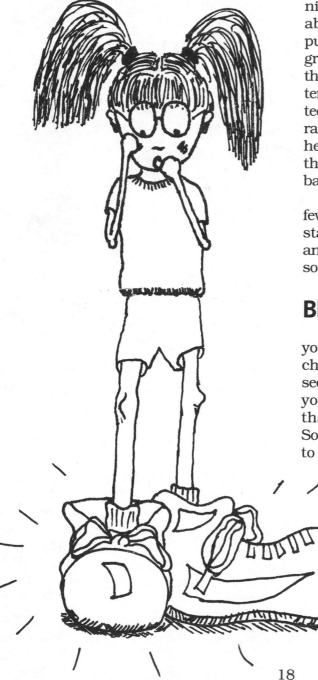

Between the age of two and the beginning of puberty, the average kid grows about two inches each year. Once the puberty growth spurt starts, this rate of growth speeds up. For the average girl, the growth spurt begins around the age of ten and continues until she's about fourteen and a half years old, with the fastest rate of growth coming sometime between her eleventh and twelfth birthday. After that, the rate of growth begins to slow back down.

It's important to remember that very few girls are exactly average, so you may start your growth spurt earlier or later and may grow faster or slower than the so-called "average" girl.

## BIGFOOT

Even before you notice a change in your height, you may notice a dramatic change in your foot size. If it suddenly seems that you outgrow your shoes before you can even begin to wear them out, that's a sign that puberty is starting. Some girls worry that their feet are going to keep growing at this rapid rate and they'll wind up with giant-sized feet. If you've worried about this, you can relax. Your feet won't keep growing like this. Feet start growing first and grow fast, but then they slow down. Your feet usually reach their adult size and stop growing before you reach your adult height.

# Growth In Girls

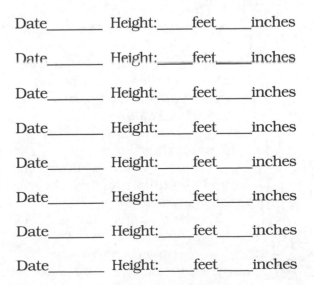

| Age | 10 | 11 | 12 | 13 | 14 | 16 | 18 |
|---|---|---|---|---|---|---|---|
| Average Height | 4'6" | 4'9" | 4'11" | 5'2" | 5'3" | 5'4" | 5'4" |
| Range of Heights (90% of girls) | 4'2" to 4'11" | 4'4" to 5'2" | 4'6" to 5'5" | 4'9" to 5'7" | 4'10" to 5'8" | 5'0" to 5'8" | 5'0" to 5'9" |

This chart shows the average height for girls at various ages between 10 and 18. Because few girls are exactly average, you may be taller or shorter than the average given in the chart. The chart also gives a "range of heights" for each age group. Ninety percent (90%) of girls (90 out of every 100) at the given age will be between the two heights shown in the chart. However, 10% of girls will be outside the ranges given. For example, 90% of 10-year-old girls are between 4'2" and 4'11" tall; 5% will be less than 4'2" tall and 5% will be more than 4'11" tall.

Keep track of your own growth by measuring yourself every 3-6 months and recording your height in the spaces provided.

## Your Growth Record

Date_____ Height:_____feet_____inches

Date_____ Height:_____feet_____inches

Date_____ Height:_____feet_____inches

Date_____ Height:_____feet_____inches

Date_____ Height:_____feet_____inches

Date_____ Height:_____feet_____inches

Date_____ Height:_____feet_____inches

Date_____ Height:_____feet_____inches

# TALL TALES

Being taller than the rest of your friends (including the boys) isn't always easy. It's hard to laugh when you hear "How's the weather up there?" for the hundredth time. Does it help to know that many women athletes and fashion models say that being tall is the best thing that ever happened to them? (Not all of them felt that way when they were your age though.)

You might like to know the kinds of things girls say about being tall:

● *I've always been the tallest in my class and I like it. My older sister was even taller than me when she was my age and she is the prettiest girl I know. Her boyfriend is shorter than she is but they don't care.*

● *Everyone teases me because I'm so tall. I'm always late for class because I wait in the bathroom until there aren't so many people in the halls. I hate getting marked late all the time.*

● *I saw a picture of myself all scrunched up trying to look shorter and I looked pretty dumb. Now I stand up straight but I still wish I wasn't so tall.*

● *I grew so fast that now all my skirts are short the way I wanted them in the first place! My best friend is kind of short and she's jealous.*

The fact is, you can't do much about your height, but you can do plenty about the way you deal with it. So, stand tall and walk proud!

# SHORT STORIES

Let's face it—people think little things are cute. Babies are cute. Fuzzy little dogs that fit on your lap are cute. And, if you are short, chances are you've been called cute too. But there are probably a dozen other things you would rather have people notice about you. You can't change your height, but you can still be all those other things you want to be. You don't have to be six feet tall to be a good friend. There are no height requirements when it comes to being funny or smart or a good athlete. Think about the things you like about being short.

Here's what other girls say about being short:

● *I'm small and I'm a very fast runner. My cousin used to call me runt and make me cry. But I won all-city honors in track this year. They don't call me runt anymore.*

● *I'm the shortest one in my class and I look like a baby compared to the other girls. My friends wear a little make-up but my mother says it just make me look foolish. I hate that.*

● *I guess everyone in my family is kind of short. I can't imagine what it would be like to be tall. I don't think I'd like it.*

# Test Your

# I.Q.

## with This

# P.Q.

## (Puberty Quiz)

**True** **False**

___ ___ **1.** The growth spurt happens at different ages for different girls, and is more noticeable in some girls than in others.

___ ___ **2.** Boys go through a growth spurt too, but theirs usually starts later and lasts longer than girls'.

___ ___ **3.** If you are on the short side before your growth spurt, you will be short as an adult too.

___ ___ **4.** The average 11-year-old girl is taller than the average 11-year-old boy.

___ ___ **5.** Girls start their growth spurts before they begin to menstruate.

___ ___ **6.** The growth spurt affects the bones in your legs and upper body before it affects your feet.

___ ___ **7.** Following her first menstrual period, the"average" girl grows another 2½ to 3 inches before she reaches her adult height and stops growing.

___ ___ **8.** The lower body (legs) start the growth spurt before the upper body (trunk).

Turn to the next page to see how well you did!

# ANSWERS

**1. True.** Girls may start their growth spurts as young as nine and a half years of age or not until they're fifteen. A girl may grow only a few inches, or she may grow as much as several inches.

**2. True.** Boys' growth spurts usually start later and last longer than girls'.

**3. False.** This isn't always the case. Sometimes a girl who is short will wind up being the tallest in her class because she grows so much during her growth spurt.

**4. True.** This is because the average girl starts her growth spurt two years before the average boy starts his. But, eventually, boys catch up and generally wind up being taller than girls.

**5. True.** In fact, by the time girls start to menstruate, their growth spurts have usually peaked and their rate of growth is slowing down.

**6. False.** It's the other way around— feet first.

**7. True.** But, remember, few girls are exactly average. It might be more helpful for you to know that 99 out of 100 girls will add between $1\frac{1}{8}$ and $4\frac{3}{4}$ inches to their height following their first periods.

**8. True.** And, the legs grow more than the trunk as well.

# Back Talk

Scoliosis is a condition in which the backbone curves to one side or the other. It's most common in girls who are going through the puberty growth spurt.

If scoliosis is not treated, there may be permanent curving of the spine, which can limit physical activity. The good news is that it is correctable, especially when it is caught early.

The symptoms include: an S-shaped curve to your spine when you bend over; uneven shoulders and/or hips; and shoulder blades that stick out more than normal. Mild cases may only require special exercises. In more severe cases, it may be necessary to wear a back brace for a time. In the most serious cases, an operation may be required, although doctors are now experimenting with treatments that don't require an operation.

The earlier scoliosis is diagnosed, the better. So the next time you see your doctor or school nurse, ask him/her to check you out.

## The Thigh Bone's Connected to the Hip Bone...

But if you have slipped capital femoral epiphysis, the growing end of the thigh bone (femur) is displaced from its normal location atop the femur. The condition occurs just before or during a period of rapid growth. Though more common in boys, the condition does occur to girls going through the puberty growth spurt, particularly those who are overweight.

Symptoms include pain in the knee and/or thigh, pain in the hip and/or groin, a "click" in the hip, and in some cases, a limp. If you have symptoms, particularly if you have a limp, see your doctor right away. The problem is treated by a surgical operation and the earlier it's treated, the better.

# Growing Pains

If you've had muscle pains in the legs and thighs that come and go, then you know what growing pains are. In girls, growing pains usually occur between the ages of five and thirteen and are especially common in ten- and eleven-year-olds. The pains are most likely to occur in the late afternoon and evening. They are most often felt behind the knee, in the thighs, or along the shins, but may also affect the arms, back, groin, shoulders, and ankles. No one knows for certain what causes the pain. Some doctors think it's due to strain as a result of the bones growing faster than the muscles.

You should discuss the pains with your doctor (just to make sure the pain isn't something serious). But growing pains do not require medical treatment. The pains will disappear on their own. Meanwhile, massages, a heating pad, and non-aspirin pain reliever should take care of the problem.

# Your Changing Figure

The puberty growth spurt causes your pelvic bones to enlarge, in particular, to become broader. In addition, fat pads grow on your hips and thighs. Thus, your hips widen, and in comparison, your waist seems narrower. These changes, along with your developing breasts, give you a more womanly figure.

The proportions your body also change. What's that mean? Simply that certain parts of our bodies grow more than others. Take, for example, the head. The overall size doesn't change much, but as babies our heads account for about 1/4 the total length of our bodies, whereas in adulthood our heads are only about 1/6 of our total height. That's because our legs

and the trunk of the body (the part between our necks and the top of our legs) grow more than our heads. At birth a baby's legs account for only 1/3 of the total body length. During puberty, the legs grow more than either the trunk or the head, and by adulthood, our legs account for about 1/2 of our height.

# Your Changing Face

The bones in your face are also affected by the puberty growth spurt, becoming both longer and wider. The greatest increase is in the length, and there is an overall change in the proportions of your face.

Your mouth widens, your lips become fuller, and your forehead higher and wider. The entire face lengthens, but the greatest increase is in the lower portion. As a result, your chin juts out more, and the overall effect is that your face is narrower and less pudgy than when you were a kid. Your nose also gets longer and wider. It may reach its adult size before the rest of the facial features, so you may look as if your nose is too big for your face until the rest of your features catch up.

In some girls, these changes are quite dramatic, while in others, they are less noticeable. Because you see yourself in the mirror each day, even dramatic changes may not be real obvious to you. But the exercise on the next page will help you see how your face changes.

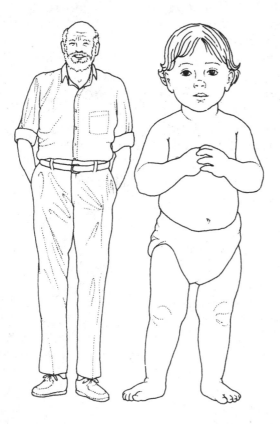

*If our proportions didn't change — if all parts of our bodies grew the same amount as we matured — we'd wind up looking like giant babies!*

# Face Match-Ups

Just to give you an idea of how much faces can change during puberty we gathered together some "before and after puberty" pictures. See if you can guess which kid turned into which adult by drawing a line connecting the pictures that go together.

Your face will change too! Of course, you may not notice these changes because you see yourself in the mirror each day. But if you do the exercise on the next page, you'll see what we mean.

1.      2.      3.

a.      b.      c.

Answers: Number 1 grew up to be b.; number 2 grew up to be c.; number 3 grew up to be a.

# PICTURE YOURSELF CHANGING

Paste in photos of yourself taken every six months or so. It'll be easier to see how much you've changed if you use the same camera and stand about the same distance from the camera for each picture. Photos from a coin-operated booth are great for showing the changes in your face. Or you might use photos that show your whole body.

Each time you add another photo to the page, write the date the picture was taken underneath it.

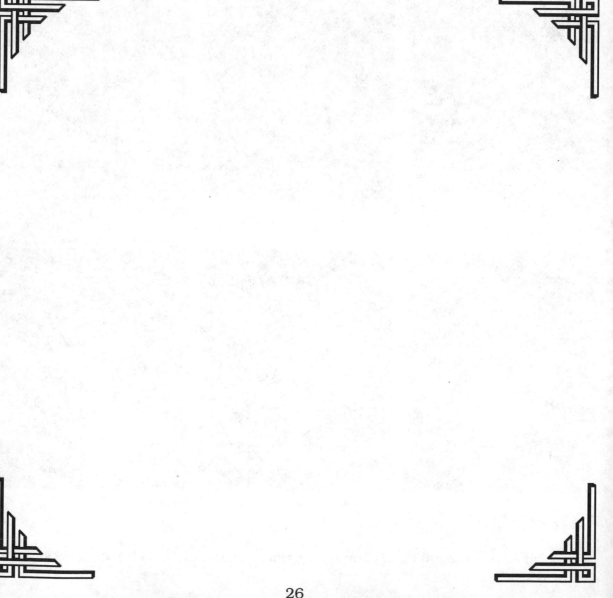

# A
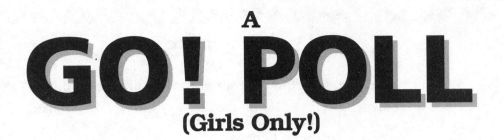
# GO! POLL
## (Girls Only!)

GO! *(short for Girls Only!), a national magazine for girls your age, polled its readers, asking them to answer the questions listed below. Now it's your turn. Write your answers in the space provided. Then read the poll results to find out how you compare to girls from all across the country.*

- **If you could change anything about yourself, what would it be?**

  ❑ **nothing**　❑ **looks**　❑ **weight**　❑ **athletic ability**　❑ **intelligence**

- **What do you like most about yourself?** _____

  _____

  _____

- **Are you happy?** ❑ **yes**　❑ **no**

- **Any other comments?** _____

  _____

  _____

## Poll Results

Over 5,000 girls responded to *GO!* Magazine's poll. A majority of them said they were really pretty happy with their lives:
- "I think I'm beautiful and should be on a soap opera."
- "I'm black and proud of who I am."

But, some teens weren't entirely happy:
- "I'm ugly and overweight. All of my friends have boyfriends except me, and it makes me sad."
- "I wish that people liked you for what's inside—not how you look." "Sometimes I'm sad, but everyone is, right?"

Turn the page to find out the final tally of the poll results.

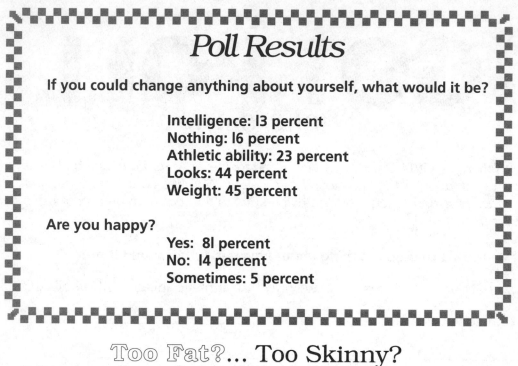

## Poll Results

**If you could change anything about yourself, what would it be?**

Intelligence: 13 percent
Nothing: 16 percent
Athletic ability: 23 percent
Looks: 44 percent
Weight: 45 percent

**Are you happy?**

Yes: 81 percent
No: 14 percent
Sometimes: 5 percent

## Too Fat?... Too Skinny?
## The "Right" Weight For You

Almost half of the girls in the *GO!* poll wanted to change their weight. Does that mean that nearly half of these girls were too fat or too skinny?

No! Most girls your age are neither under- nor overweight. Although there are some girls who do have a real weight problem, the majority of girls are at the right weight for their body type and stage of development.

|  | Yes | No |
|---|---|---|
| ◆ Do you think you're too fat ? | ❏ | ❏ |
| ◆ Do you go on crash diets? | ❏ | ❏ |
| ◆ Do you skip meals as a way of dieting? | ❏ | ❏ |
| ◆ Does this sound like you? | ❏ | ❏ |

◆ Does this sound like you?
*I tell myself I've got to go on a diet. Then if I eat, I feel guilty. But if I don't eat, I get hungry. My solution? I eat all I want and feel guilty all the time.*

If your answer to any of these questions is "yes," pay special attention to the next few pages of this workbook!

# What's Your Basic Body Type?

**A**lthough dieting and exercise can change the shape of our bodies to some extent, we each have a basic body type that can't be changed, no matter how much dieting and exercising we do. The three most common body types are shown here. Read the descriptions of each type and put a check mark next to the one that most closely describes your body type.

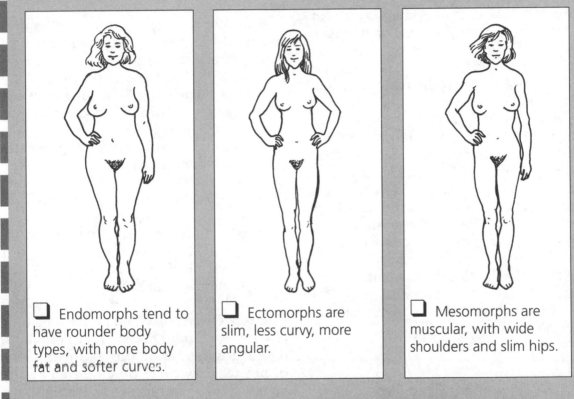

❑ Endomorphs tend to have rounder body types, with more body fat and softer curves.

❑ Ectomorphs are slim, less curvy, more angular.

❑ Mesomorphs are muscular, with wide shoulders and slim hips.

If you're an endomorph, it's important for you to know that you may be at a weight that is the perfectly healthy, ideal weight for you, yet look heavier than your friends or classmates who are the same weight as you but who are ectomorphs.

You also need to know that the super-skinny models in magazines and on TV, besides being underweight, may have a more angular body type than yours. If that's the case, you can never really look like they do, no matter how much weight you try to lose. So, before you jump to the conclusion that you're "too fat" (or, for that matter, "too thin"), take your basic body type into account. You may be just the right for your body type!

# Puberty & Pounds

Girls your age sometimes get the mistaken idea that they're "too fat" because they've suddenly put on a lot of weight. But, you're supposed to gain weight during puberty!

Between the ages of ten and fourteen, girls typically gain about forty pounds. This weight gain may happen quickly, so that a girl gains fifteen pounds in a year (or, in even less time). Or, the weight gain may be spread out over two or three years.

You'll also be going through the height growth spurt and getting taller. The increase in your weight and the increase in your height don't always happen at the exactly the same time. It's a seesaw kind of thing. There may be times when you're putting on the pounds faster than you're adding inches and vice versa. So there may be times when you're temporarily chubbier or thinner than is usual for you.

Girls who are having a chubby period sometimes freak out and decide they have to start dieting or they'll be fat forever. But dieting can be hazardous to your health, especially during puberty!

# Dumb Diets/ Dangerous Diets

Some diets are just plain dumb. You know the kind we mean—the ones that claim the amazing watermelon diet will "melt the pounds away" or promise that you can eat banana splits three times a day and lose twenty pounds a week. These sort of fad diets always sound great, but diets where you only eat certain foods deprive your body of the vitamins, minerals, and other nutrients it needs. Besides being dumb, these diets can also be dangerous. They can really wreck your health, causing dizziness and fatigue, making you feel tired and weak, drying out your skin and scalp, and maybe even making your hair fall out.

In order for menstruation to happen you need to have a certain amount of fat in your body. Severe dieting can keep a girl from getting her period in the first place, or cause a girl who is already menstruating to "miss" periods or to stop menstruating altogether.

In addition, two very serious health problems—anorexia and bulimia—often begin with a constant round of dieting during the preteen or teen years. (See box, next page).

Dieting during puberty can also stunt your growth. To grow properly, your bones need plenty of calcium, as well as other minerals, vitamins, and nutrients. Studies have shown that teens who put themselves on strict diets are not only underweight, but shorter than normal. In one study, some of the younger teens began to grow once they started eating properly, but some of the older teens didn't. (And, by the way, none of the teens got fat once they began eating regular diets!)

It's best to stay away from fad diets. In fact, unless your doctor tells you that you have a weight problem, it's best to forget about dieting during puberty. Instead, just follow some basic commonsense rules. Eat a variety of foods: fruits, veggies, milk or cheese, meat or fish, and grains (found in cereal or pasta). If you're hungry, definitely go back for seconds, but choose fruits and veggies for your "seconds." Stay away from snack foods. Cut down on sweets and desserts. Cut back on fats such as butter and fried food. Get some form of exercise at least three times a week. Drink at least eight glasses of water a day. If you follow these rules, you won't need to diet— you'll be at the exactly right weight for you!

## Anorexia & Bulimia

Anorexia and bulimia are eating disorders. A person who is anorexic hardly eats anything at all and may also do strenuous physical exercise to further reduce her weight. Although an anorexic has starved herself to the point where she's just skin and bones, when she looks in the mirror she sees herself as fat. People who are bulimic take laxatives and make themselves vomit after eating to avoid gaining any weight. They often go on eating binges, stuffing themselves with food, and then vomit. Bulimics are also prone to "over exercise." But unlike anorexics, bulimics are usually average or even overweight.

Bulimia and anorexia are very serious problems. Bulimia can cause dental, stomach, bowel, heart, and circulatory disorders and may lead to early death. Anorexics may lose so much weight that they have to be hospitalized and fed intravenously (through needles) or through tubes placed up the nose and down the throat and into the stomach in order to keep them alive. Anorexia can lead to heart problems and other serious diseases and is fatal in 20% of the cases. There is hope, though. Counseling can help people overcome these problems but the chances of success are much greater if the problem is recognized and treatment is begun during the preteen and teen years.

If you have an eating disorder (or think you might), or if you simply want more information, you can call the Eating Disorders Awareness and Prevention hotline twenty-four hours a day, seven days a week. The toll free (no-cost) number to call is 1-800-931-2237. You don't have to give your name, and the call won't appear on your phone bill.

# Your Looks: What You Like/What You Don't Like

Now that your body is changing, how do you feel about your body and the way you look? What are the things you like? What don't you like? In the space below make a list of the things you like and don't like.

You don't have to fill in all the spaces. The two lists don't need to be the same length, but spend about the same amount of time on each list.

### *What I like*

_____

_____

_____

_____

_____

_____

_____

### *What I don't like*

_____

_____

_____

_____

_____

_____

_____

• • • • • • • • • • • • • • • • • • • • • • • • • • • • • • • • • • • • • • • • • • • •

If your "likes" list is longer than your "don't likes" list, good for you! If not, join the crowd. Most of us (girls and women) find it harder to think up things that we do like about our bodies, which isn't too surprising if you think about it. Everywhere we look—television, movies, billboards, magazines—we see smiling glamorous women who are usually tall, thin (very), large-breasted, and long-legged, with high cheekbones, tiny waists, and not a single dimple of fat or bulge anywhere. They may not come right out and say it, but the message is clear: "if you looked like this, life would be great." But the truth is, these images of the "perfect" looking woman are designed to make us feel insecure about ourselves so that we'll buy the latest makeup, hairdye, nail polish, or whatever else they're selling. Most of us don't look like that, and we never will. We come in a variety of wonderful shapes and sizes. That's what makes us so special, and it's too bad that images in the media are able to make us feel bad about ourselves.

# PART 3

# A GIRL SPROUT'S GUIDE TO PUBIC HAIRS & BREASTS

The growth spurt is one of the early signs of puberty. The appearance of curly pubic hairs growing on the vulva is another early sign. For some girls this is the first sign of puberty. For others, the first sign comes when the areola, the ring of colored tissue around the nipple, gets larger and the breasts begin to swell and to stand out from the chest.

The breasts enlarge because milk-producing gland tissues, cushioned by layers of fat tissue, begin to form under the nipples. Your breasts aren't ready to make milk yet, and they won't be ready until you've had a child. But your body is getting ready for a time in your life when you may decide to have a child and want to breastfeed your baby.

No one can say for sure when a girl will begin to develop breasts and start growing pubic hair. For most girls, these changes start to happen between the ages of nine and eleven. But some girls start when they are younger than this, and others not until they are older.

Being earlier or later to start than other girls doesn't mean there's something wrong with you. It simply means your body is developing at its own special rate.

This section will help you learn more about how, when, and why these changes happen.

# Which Stage Are You In?

Doctors have divided pubic hair growth into the five stages shown here. You may be in one stage or in between one stage and the next. Put a check in the box next to the stage that most closely matches your pubic hair growth.

☐ **Stage 1** – In the childhood stage there isn't any coarse, curly pubic hair.

☐ **Stage 2** – This stage starts when you grow your first pubic hairs. There are only a few hairs at first and they may be only slightly curly.

☐ **Stage 3** – The pubic hair gets curlier and may darken in color. There is more of it than in Stage 2.

☐ **Stage 4** – The pubic hair may continue to get darker. It's curlier and covers an even wider area.

☐ **Stage 5** – In the final, adult stage, the pubic hair usually grows in an upside down triangle pattern, though in some women it grows up toward the belly button or out toward the thighs.

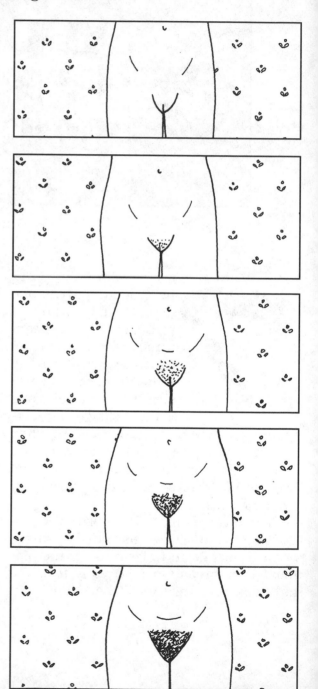

# Test Your
# I.Q.
## with This
# P.Q.
### (Puberty Quiz)

| True | False | |
|------|-------|---|
| ____ | ____ | **1.** A girl's pubic hair is always the same color as the hair on her head. |
| ____ | ____ | **2.** Most girls don't begin to menstruate until they've reached Stage 4 of pubic hair development. |
| ____ | ____ | **3.** Most girls reach Stage 3 of pubic hair growth between the ages of eleven and thirteen. |
| ____ | ____ | **4.** As a woman grows older, her pubic hair may turn gray. |
| ____ | ____ | **5.** If a girl is fourteen years old and hasn't begun to develop pubic hair or breasts, she should have a check-up with her doctor. |
| ____ | ____ | **6.** Plucking your pubic hairs will keep them from growing. |
| ____ | ____ | **7.** The amount of pubic hair a woman has depends on her racial, ethnic, and family background. |
| ____ | ____ | **8.** If a girl finds loose pubic hairs on her sheets, pajamas, or under clothes, she should consult her doctor. |
| ____ | ____ | **9.** Just as eyelashes help protect sensitive eye tissues, so pubic hairs help protect the sensitive tissues of the vulva. |
| ____ | ____ | **10.** Some girls reach Stage 5 when they're only twelve years old; others not until they're seventeen or older. |

Turn the page to see how you did!

# ANSWERS

**1. False.** Pubic hair isn't always the same color as the hair on your head.

**2. True.** The majority of girls have their first period while they are in Stage 4 of pubic hair growth. However, there are also many girls who have their first period while they're in Stage 3, and some don't have theirs until they reach Stage 5.

**3. True.** The average is eleven to thirteen years old, but some girls reach this stage when they're only ten and others not until they're fifteen or older.

**4. True.** Like the hair on your head, pubic hair may turn gray when you get older.

**5. True.** But there are many perfectly normal, healthy girls who don't go through puberty until they're older. Girls who haven't shown any pubic hair or breast development by the age of fourteen should get checked out by a doctor, just in case they have a medical problem that needs treatment.

**6. False.** If you pluck your pubic hairs, they'll just grow back. Besides, plucking these hairs hurts and could also lead to infection.

**7. True.** Women from certain racial and ethnic groups tend to have more pubic hair than women from other groups. A woman's personal family background (what she inherits from her parents) determines how much pubic hair she has.

**8. False.** It's completely normal to find hairs from your head on your hairbrush, or on your sweaters, coats, etc., and it's also normal for pubic hairs to fall out and be replaced by new hairs.

**9. True.** Our vulvas are very sensitive, and pubic hairs help to protect them.

**10. True.** The "average" age is fifteen, but a girl may be as young as twelve or seventeen or older before she reaches the adult stage of pubic hair growth.

# Thoughts & Feelings:
# PUBIC HAIR

I was taking a bath and I noticed three little curly hairs growing down there. I started yelling for my mom to come and see.

—Carmen, age 12

I didn't know what they were, so I got the tweezers and pulled them out. Pretty soon, they grew back...and then there were more and more of them. So I figured they must be okay.

—Stephanie, age 13

I remember when I first saw that my pubic hairs were growing. I thought, "Oh, no, I don't want this to start happening to me yet.

—Melissa, age 13

# HOW DO YOU FEEL?

Use the space below to freewrite about your first pubic hairs. When did you first notice them? Where were you? What went through your head? How did you feel about this change? (P.S. If you've forgotten how to freewrite, see page 9.)

_____

_____

_____

_____

# Which Stage Are You In?

Doctors have divided breast development into the five stages shown here. You may be in one of these stages or in between one stage and the next. Put a check in the box next to the stage that most closely matches your breast growth.

❑ **Stage 1** – In the childhood stage, the breasts are flat. Only the nipple is raised. The areola is still small in size.

❑ **Stage 2** – Breast development begins. The nipple and the areola get larger and darker in color, and a small, flat, buttonlike "breast bud" develops under each nipple.

❑ **Stage 3** – The nipple and areola continue to get larger and darker in color. The breasts enlarge and may be rather cone-shaped and pointy in this stage.

❑ **Stage 4** – The areola and nipple form a separate little mound so that they stick out above the rest of the breast. Not all girls go through this stage.

❑ **Stage 5** – In the final stage the breasts have a fuller, more rounded adult shape.

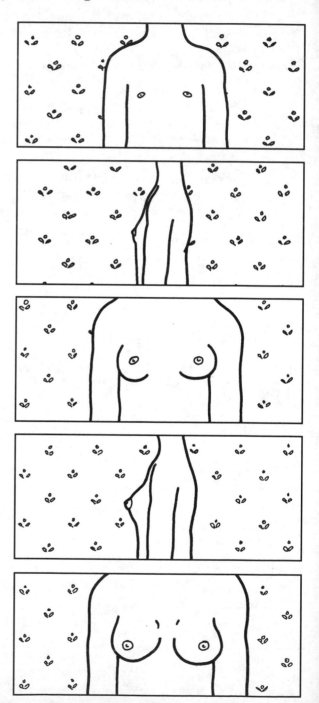

# Test Your

# I.Q.

## with This

# P.Q.

### (Puberty Quiz)

**True  False**

\_\_\_\_ \_\_\_\_ **1.** A girl whose breasts start to develop at an early age will reach her adult breast size sooner and have larger breasts than a girl who starts to develop later.

\_\_\_\_ \_\_\_\_ **2.** Both of your breasts will start to develop at about the same time, and they will be about the same size.

\_\_\_\_ \_\_\_\_ **3.** Your breasts may feel tender, sore, or even downright painful when they are developing.

\_\_\_\_ \_\_\_\_ **4.** If your nipples are stroked or touched, if they get cold, or if you have "sexy" feelings or thoughts, your nipples may become stiff and erect.

\_\_\_\_ \_\_\_\_ **5.** You may be in one stage of breast development and a different stage of pubic hair growth.

\_\_\_\_ \_\_\_\_ **6.** Most girls don't have their first menstrual period until they've reached Stage 3 or Stage 4 of breast development.

\_\_\_\_ \_\_\_\_ **7.** If you find tiny hairs growing around your areola, you should pluck them out.

\_\_\_\_ \_\_\_\_ **8.** There are exercises you can do to make your breasts larger.

\_\_\_\_ \_\_\_\_ **9.** It usually takes about three to four years for a girls breasts to reach the fully developed, adult stage.

\_\_\_\_ \_\_\_\_ **10.** If one or both of a girl's nipples sinks into the areola instead of sticking out, she should see a doctor.

Turn to the next page to see how well you did!

# ANSWERS

**1. False.** How early or late a girl starts to develop doesn't have anything to do with how fast she develops or how large her breasts will be.

**2. False.** Although each of a grown woman's breasts are just about the same size, a girl whose breasts are just developing may find that one starts to grow before the other or is larger.

**3. True.** Many girls experience some tenderness or even outright pain when their breasts are developing.

**4. True.** Nipples are very sensitive, and touching, coldness, or sexual arousal can all cause your nipples to become erect.

**5. True.** You won't necessarily be at the same stages of pubic hair and breast development. For example, a girl might be in Stage 3 of breast development and Stage 2 or Stage 4 of pubic hair growth.

**6. True.** Most girls start to menstruate during the later part of Stage 3 or during Stage 4.

**7. False.** Some women do grow tiny hairs around their areola, but it's not a good idea to pluck them. Plucking can

be painful and can lead to an infection. Besides, the hairs will probably grow right back.

**8. False.** Your breasts are made up of fat tissue and milk glands, and no amount of exercise can make them larger. You can do exercises to make the muscles of your chest wall thicker, the way weightlifters do. Thicker chest walls will push your breasts, making them appear larger, but you can't actually increase the size of the breast itself through exercise.

**9. True.** On the average it takes about three to four years for a girl's breasts to fully develop, but not everyone is average. Some girls are fully developed in just a year and a half; for others it takes several years from the time they first start to develop.

**10. False.** This is called "an inverted nipple." It's very common and doesn't cause any problems. In fact, as a girl continues to develop, the inverted nipple may stick out.

# THOUGHTS & FEELINGS: BREASTS

I'm flat-chested, and the only thing that makes me mad is when they tell those jokes. Here's one of them: "I have a joke that will make your tits fall off—Oh, I see you've already heard it." Then they go off laughing.

—Essie, age 13

Grown-ups are always saying things like, "Oh, you're really popping out," or "You're sure bursting out all over," and sometimes my breasts feel sore, like they really are about to burst, so I wondered.

—Leah, age 12

I'm kind of flat. Do you think it's silly for me to want a bra?

—Kelly, age 11

I was so happy when my breasts started growing. I was always showing them off to my mom and little sister.

—Cassandra, age 14

# HOW DO *YOU* FEEL?

Complete the sentences below.

Compared to other girls my age, I'm developing (*circle one*) **faster, slower, about average.**

This makes me feel _____

When I get (got) my first bra, I _____

_____

When I think about my breasts, I _____

_____

# The Growth and Development of My Favorite Person

Use the entries on these pages to keep a record of your growth and development as you progress through the various stages of puberty. Every three to six months come back to this page and fill in another box. (P.S. The information recorded here will be really helpful when you get to the exercise in Part 6 on page 89.)

DATE:_____ BREAST STAGE#_____ PUBIC HAIR #_____

*The most important thing in my life right now is*

DATE:_____ BREAST STAGE#_____ PUBIC HAIR #_____

*I am looking forward to*

DATE:_____ BREAST STAGE#_____ PUBIC HAIR #_____

*I worry about*

DATE:_____ BREAST STAGE#_____ PUBIC HAIR #_____

*My parents would like me to*

DATE:_____ BREAST STAGE#_____ PUBIC HAIR #_____

*I secretly have a crush on*

DATE:_____ BREAST STAGE#_____ PUBIC HAIR #_____

*When I'm grown I plan to*

DATE:_____ BREAST STAGE#_____ PUBIC HAIR #_____

*The woman I admire most is*

DATE:_____ BREAST STAGE#_____ PUBIC HAIR #_____

*My friends describe me as*

DATE:_____ BREAST STAGE#_____ PUBIC HAIR #_____

*One thing that really bugs me is*

DATE:_____ BREAST STAGE#_____ PUBIC HAIR #_____

*The best thing that happened to me lately is*

DATE:_____ BREAST STAGE#_____ PUBIC HAIR #_____

*I feel good about myself when*

# What Would You Do?

**1.** Jan is thirteen years old and lives with her father. Her breasts have started to develop and she feels she is ready to start wearing a bra. She and her dad get along all right, but she still feels too embarrassed to talk to him about it.

What suggestions do you have for Jan?

_____

_____

_____

_____

**2.** Even though Donna's breasts have really begun to develop, she's not so hot on the idea of wearing a bra. She thinks they're uncomfortable, and she's seen the boys at school make a big deal out of when a girl wears a bra. Her mom has been putting the pressure on for a couple of months. Now she's insisting that Donna go shopping for a bra.

Can you think of something for Donna to do?

_____

_____

_____

_____

**3.** Toni lives with her mother and four sisters and brothers. She is in junior high and feels like it is time to buy her first bra.

Her mom agrees, but tells Toni she will not be able to afford to shop for her for at least two months. Toni's older sister tried to help out, but her bras were too large.

Do you have some advice for Toni?

_____

_____

_____

_____

**4.** Gloria has not yet started to develop, so she doesn't really need a bra. But most of her friends wear bras and she wants to at least get one of these training bras that you can wear even if you're not at all developed. She's asked her mother a few times and even said she would buy it with her own allowance. But, her mom just says, "You're too young," or "This is really not the time to talk about it."

What can Gloria do?

_____

_____

_____

_____

Now compare your answers to the answers other people have given.

**1.** Jan can:
✗ Ask a female relative—an aunt, grandmother, or cousin to talk to her father for her.

44

✗ Write him a note.

✗ Drop some hints—put up a magazine ad of bras on her bedroom wall.

✗ Tough it out! "This is kind of embarrassing dad, but..." (Her dad might have been waiting for her to say something all along!)

✗ Go get one on her own.

**2.** Donna can:

✗ Talk to her mom and try and find out why her mom wants her to wear one.

✗ Compromise—Try wearing a bra to school and taking it off when she gets home. She might start getting used to it.

✗ Try another style, such as the tube or sport bra that will be more comfortable and less noticeable.

**3.** Toni can:

✗ Ask for a bra for her birthday if it is coming up soon.

✗ Ask a close friend or relative if she can borrow a bra.

✗ Look in the local discount for a sale or bargain price.

✗ Do some small jobs (babysitting or gardening chores) for neighbors or relatives and earn the money herself.

✗ Take in one of the hand-me-downs from her sister.

**4.** Gloria can:

✗ Ask her mother when would be a good time to talk about it.

✗ Tell her mom she feels left out from her group of friends.

✗ Write her mom a note, or even write a story about a girl who wants a training bra and give the story to her mother.

✗ Ask an aunt, a grandmother, or another relative to talk with her mom for her.

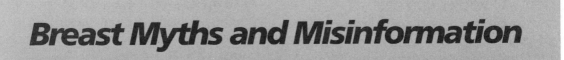

# Breast Myths and Misinformation

**C**an you separate fact from fiction in the six statements below? Only one of these six is true. Put a check mark in front of the correct statement.

1. Women with large breasts produce more breast milk than women with small breasts.
2. If your mother has big breasts you will too; if she has small ones, so will you.
3. Women with big breasts are sexier than women with small breasts.
4. If you sleep on your stomach, your breasts won't grow as quickly.
5. Wearing a training bra will help your breasts grow properly.
6. Boys' breasts also swell and get bigger during puberty.

Answer: Only statement #6 is correct. Seven out of ten boys experience some temporary swelling and tenderness of the breasts during puberty.

# Buying a Bra

Before you go to buy your first bra, you'll need to determine your correct bra size using a tape measure, as described below.

Bras come in sizes like 34C, 28B, 30AA. The first part—the number—is the band size. The second part—the letter—is the cup size.

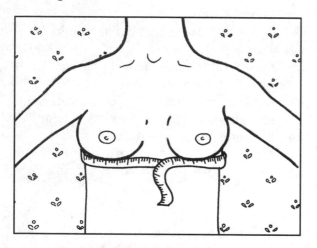

## I. TO FIGURE YOUR BAND SIZE:

Wrap the tape measure around your chest just below your breasts and underneath your arms as shown here. Be careful to keep the tapemeasure level. You may want to have someone help you. Write your measurement here _____

Then, add six inches
to that number _____ + 6 _____

TOTAL _____

○ If your total is an even number*, then that number is your band size.
○ If your total is an odd number, you'll need to subtract 1 inch to get your band size.

Example: If you measure 27 inches, you'd add 6 inches and your total would be 33 inches. Since 33 is an odd number, you'd need to subtract one inch, giving you a size of 32 inches.

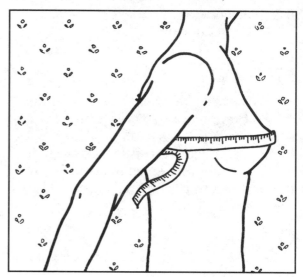

## II. TO FIGURE YOUR CUP SIZE:

Wrap the tape measure around your chest again, this time at the fullest part of your breasts, across the nipples as shown above.

Write that number here _____.
○ If this number is less than your band size, your cup size is AAA.
○ If this number is the same as your band size, your cup size is AA.
○ If this number is one inch more than your band size, you'll wear an A.
○ If this number is two inches more than your band size, your cup size is a B. If it's three inches more, it's a C, and so on through cup sizes D, DD, and E. Larger sizes can be purchased in specialty stores.

* * * * * * * * * * * * * * * * * * * * * * * * * * * * * * *

*Even numbers end in 0, 2, 4, 6, 8; odd numbers end in 1, 3, 5, 7, or 9.

# Choosing Your Bra

There are many different styles. If you haven't really begun to develop, but would like a bra anyhow (which is perfectly fine), there are one-size-fits-all bras. Made of a stretchy material, they are basically halter-tops cut to look like a bra. Bras with AA or AAA cups are often called "training bras," and if you've just begun to develop, you'll want to start with one of these. If your breasts aren't real big, you can wear a natural bra. These are comfortable and provide support. An underwire bra is great for girls with larger breasts because it offers plenty of support. The maximizer or padded bra has some padding to make your chest look a little fuller than it really is.

Remember to try on the bra before you buy it because different styles fit differently. Also, bras cost ten dollars or more and they're usually not returnable. If you feel embarrassed about getting help from the sales lady, ask someone to come along with you to the store. Your mom, older sister, or friend will be able to help you out.

## Puberty On Planet Zeebo

"Planet Zeebo is a lot like Earth — the same air, same gravity, and even the same flavors of ice cream!" says sex educator Eartha Sewell.

And if you think that's amazing, wait till you hear this: Zeeboans not only look very much like Earthlings, but the aliens' bodies work in pretty much the same way as the human body. There is, however, one big difference — Puberty!

On Planet Zeebo, girls don't worry about when they'll get their period, what their breasts will look like, or how tall they'll be. Girls on Planet Zeebo already know all of these things. You see, on Zeebo, girls go to sleep on the night before their twelfth birthday and when they wake up they have grown-up bodies and they've started their periods! And no one worries about how they'll look because everyone is the same height, weight, shape, and they even have the same bra size!

## Puberty Zeeboan Style vs. Puberty Earth Style

Now, listen in on an interplanetary phone call (a lot more expensive than a 976 phone call) between Erma an Earthling and Zena from Zeebo...

47

Erma: Puberty is the pits on Earth. You have it so easy on Zeebo.

Erma: I'd trade you anytime. How would you like to get your first period when you least expect it—in class!?

Erma: From girl to woman in one night. Overnight respect!  Great.

Erma: Well, I think it's great that you're all the same. No one gets teased for being slower or faster to develop.

Erma: Still, when you buy your first bra, some strange bra lady you don't even know takes your measurements right in the store.

Erma: But on  Zeebo at least you know you're liked for your personality and not your looks.

Zena: Get real Earthgirl! You have it easy. You go through puberty gradually. We have to do it all in one night.

Zena: Yeah, well, 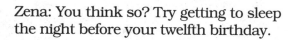 what if your mom's too chicken to talk, and one day—zammo!—you wake up in a woman's body?      Total planetary freak out!

Zena: You think so? Try getting to sleep the night before your twelfth birthday.

Zena: Oh, sure, just great.      It took me a week to find my best friend after her twelfth birthday! She got so desperate to be different that she dyed her beautiful green      hair brown.

Zena: How cool! You get to go out and buy your bras? We have to wear our mother's hand-me-downs.

Zena: At least you have your own looks.

Erma and Zena spent the next two hours going back and forth about who was having the biggest bummer (and they racked up a quarter of a million dollars in phone charges which they're going to have to pay out of their allowances...)

Who do you think has the biggest bummer? Imagine puberty on Planet Zeebo and think about how it would be different than puberty here. Then use the space below to list three good things about puberty on Zeebo and three bad things.

good things

bad things

_____

_____

_____

_____

_____

_____

Now cover up your answers. Have one of your parents or a friend read about Zeebo and list the good and bad things, too.

good things

bad things

_____

_____

_____

_____

_____

_____

Compare your answers. Were they the same or different? Did you like something they didn't? Did they like something you didn't? Which type of puberty would you each prefer? Why?

You can use your answers to all the above questions to help you with the exercise on the next page.

Invent your own planet and explain how puberty happens in your world. How is it the same or different from Planet Earth?

_____

_____

_____

_____

_____

_____

_____

_____

_____

Draw a picture to go with your imaginary planet...

# PART FOUR

# B.O. & Zits — Is Puberty The Pits?

No, puberty won't turn you into a smelly, hairy, pimply greaseball, though books, pamphlets, and videos for girls your age make it sound that way. You know the kind we mean—the ones that go on and on about "personal hygiene." They can make you feel really paranoid about B.O. (body odor), and body hair—like you'll need to shave yourself from head to toe and soak in a vat of deodorant every day. Or they make it seem that if you don't wash your face ten times a day and coat yourself with pimple cream, you'll be a permanent resident of zit city.

It's true that puberty causes changes in your skin. One result is that you have more body hair than you did as a child. Another is that perspiration (sweat) glands in the skin become more active (which means that you perspire more) and your body odor changes. Oil glands in the skin of the scalp, the face, and elsewhere in the body also become more active and you may notice that the hair on your head is more oily or that you have more pimples.

But, before you panic, read the information and try the activities and exercises in this section. They'll teach you the real facts about these changes and how to cope with them.

# Perspiration And Body Odor (Sweat And B.O.)

Remember when you were really young and you used to dread taking baths? Well, hopefully, those days are over because puberty brings changes that make regular bathing a must!

As you grow older, your sweat glands become more active, and your body chemistry changes so that you develop a more adult body odor. You perspire in the areas of your body that have more of those glands—under your arms, the palms of your hands, the bottoms of your feet, and between your legs (the vulva).

Perspiration is healthy, so let it pore! As long as you wash your body regularly and wear clean clothes, your body odor shouldn't be a problem. In many of the world's cultures, people do not use deodorants or antiperspirants, but in our culture they often do. Underarm deodorants control odor, while antiperspirants reduce wetness and help to control how much you perspire. These are available separately or can both be in the same product. Baking soda can also be used under the arms to absorb wetness and odor. It's important to remember, though, that deodorants and powders are not a substitute for soap and water.

Don't use vaginal deodorant sprays. They can irritate the sensitive skin of the vulva. Besides, an unpleasant vaginal odor could be a sign of infection. By covering up odor you could be ignoring an important signal from your body.

# Pimples and Acne

Zits, whiteheads, blackheads...if they don't sound like a lot of fun, that's because they aren't. Unfortunately, they're very common during puberty—eight out of every ten teens develop pimples and acne.

During puberty, oil glands beneath the surface of the skin enlarge and begin making increased amounts of sebum, a white, oily substance that keeps the skin moist. The extra sebum can get backed up in the ducts of the enlarged oil glands and cause whiteheads or blackheads. Both are susceptible to infection, and even normal skin bacteria can trigger an infection resulting in the red, swollen, pus-filled ducts that are officially known as pimples. The infection may break through the walls of the ducts, causing a more severe skin problem commonly known as acne. (Actually, in medical terminology, whiteheads, blackheads, and pimples are also forms of acne.)

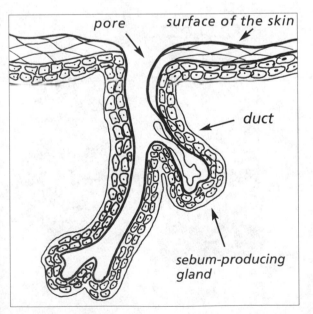

Many people have the mistaken idea that blackheads and other forms of acne are caused by tiny particles of dirt beneath the skin and that washing your face several times a day will prevent these skin problems. Not true!

When sebum comes in contact with your skin's surface it turns black and it's this, not dirt, that's responsible for blackheads. Washing your face twice a day will remove dirt and dead cells that could add to the problem. But washing only affects the surface of your skin; acne is caused by what happens under the surface of the skin. You could wash your face a hundred times a day, but it won't keep you from getting acne.

It may help to remember that girls usually outgrow these skin problems before the end of their teen years. Meanwhile, here are some tips to help you deal with zits:

○ Don't use oil-based cosmetics (they can clog the pores).

○ Don't squeeze zits or blackheads as this can cause scars. (African-American girls should be especially careful about this, see page 57.)

○ Mild and moderate cases can often be treated effectively with acne lotions and creams that are sold over-the-counter (without a doctor's prescription). Products that contain benzoyl peroxide are the most effective for pimples and acne. However, salicylic acid products are very effective for whiteheads and blackheads. Don't waste your money on non-prescription antibacterial soaps or abrasive soaps and scrubs. (African-American girls should avoid abrasives—see page 57.)

○ If over-the-counter treatments don't work, see your doctor for a number of effective medical treatments.

# Body Hair

Growing pubic hair isn't the only "hairy" change that happens. The hair all over your body is affected by puberty.

**On Your Head** – During puberty, the oil glands in your scalp are more active. Your hair is more oily and needs to be washed more often.

**Underarm Hair** – Hair starts to grow under your arms, in your armpits. Underarm hair usually appears after pubic hair and breasts have started to develop, but before the first menstrual period. However, some girls develop underarm hair before they begin to menstruate, and for some, underarm hair is among the first signs that puberty is beginning.

**Arms and Legs** – There may be more hair on your arms and legs as well, and it may be darker in color than it was during childhood. Although some of the girls who develop dark hair on their arms during puberty continue to have this hair as adults, other girls "outgrow" this as they get older.

**Other Body Hair** – Some girls develop facial hair (on the upper lip, chin, or sides of the face) and/or chest hair (hairs on the breasts, around the nipple, or between the breasts). This type of hair growth is usually an inherited characteristic, the result of a girl's ethnic and personal family background, and is completely normal. However, on occasion, this hair growth is a sign of a medical problem. If a girl does not have a family tendency to hairiness and the increase in facial and other hair has been relatively sudden or rapid, she should see her doctor, but the large majority of girls who develop facial or chest hair *do not* have an underlying medical problem.

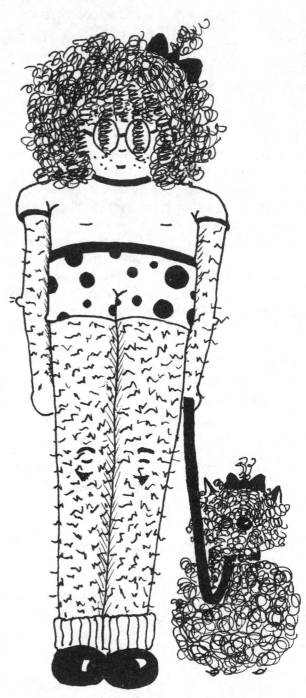

54

# THOUGHTS & FEELINGS: BODY HAIR

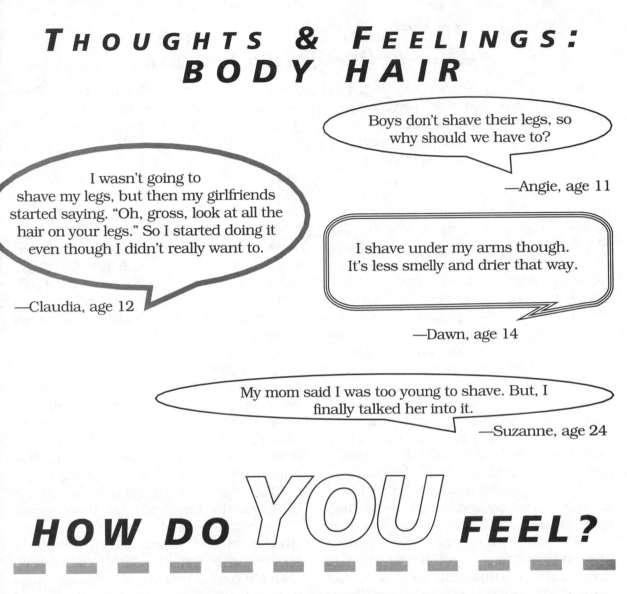

Boys don't shave their legs, so why should we have to?

—Angie, age 11

I wasn't going to shave my legs, but then my girlfriends started saying. "Oh, gross, look at all the hair on your legs." So I started doing it even though I didn't really want to.

—Claudia, age 12

I shave under my arms though. It's less smelly and drier that way.

—Dawn, age 14

My mom said I was too young to shave. But, I finally talked her into it.

—Suzanne, age 24

# HOW DO YOU FEEL?

How about you? Are you hairy or not-so-hairy? Do you remove hair from your legs, your armpits, or elsewhere? Why or why not? Use the space below to write your thoughts and feelings. (P. S. The freewriting rules are on page 9.)

_____

_____

_____

_____

# Hair Today, Gone Tomorrow:
## A Guide To Safe Hair Removal

If you want to remove body hair (and your parents say OK), you'll need to decide how to remove it. Read the following descriptions of the methods for removing hair and check any that you might use.

☐ **Shaving** – Shaving with an electric or regular blade razor cuts the hair away at the level of the skin's surface. Shaving is painless, easy-to-do, and as a rule, less irritating than other methods. But, hair regrows quickly and may look and feel as if it's darker and thicker (though it really isn't). Also, shaving can cause irritating bumps on the vulva, which can be a problem when shaving is used to remove pubic hair from the bikini area.

Never lend or borrow a razor and clean yours after each use. Shave against the direction of hair growth—upward on legs, downward (with arm raised) on underarms. Use shaving cream, lotion, or a soapy lather to cut down on "razor burn" (a painful rash caused by the razor "dragging" on the skin). Soaking in a warm or hot tub for several minutes before shaving also softens the hair and cuts down on razor burn. Putting skin powder on the legs before shaving with an electric razor makes for a closer shave. Remember that applying lotion to legs or deodorant to underarms immediately after shaving may irritate and sting.

☐ **Creams (Depilatories)** – Depilatory creams contain chemicals which dissolve the hair just below the level of the skin, making for smoother and longer-lasting hair removal than shaving. The cream is applied to the skin in the direction of hair growth and left on for a specified time. When it is wiped away, the unwanted hair is wiped off as well.

Creams can be very irritating to the skin. There are creams made for use on the face, the legs, or the bikini area, and the ones intended for the legs or bikini area should never be used on the face. Depilatories should not be used on the underarms. Be sure to follow the directions carefully and always test the product on a patch of skin before use, as depilatories are too irritating for many women.

☐ **Waxes** – Hot wax is applied to the skin, allowed to cool, and then is removed. As the wax is peeled off, the unwanted hairs are pulled out. There are also cold waxes available. (We've tried some of the cold ones and were not impressed, but maybe that was just us.)

There are different waxes for use on the legs, the face, and the bikini area. Waxes should only be used on the areas they're intended for. Though waxing removes hair for a longer period of time than shaving or creams, it is not a permanent method of hair removal. Nor is it a painless method. Although home kits are available, it's best done by a professional at a beauty or waxing salon. If you do it yourself, follow the directions carefully and do a skin patch test before using.

☐ **Bleaching** – Bleaching lightens rather than removes the hair, so it's not a good method if you have dark skin. Always use these products on the area they're intended for, and make sure you're using bleach made for use on the skin, and not laundry or hair bleach.

Although bleach is generally less irritating and safer than cream, some women find that it causes hairs to stiffen and stick straight out, so that removal becomes necessary. Women with light skin sometimes complain of an orange or yellow tinge.

Here again, it's important that you read the instructions and do a patch test before you use the bleach.

☐ **Tweezing** – Plucking is best done during or right after a bathing when hairs are soft. Tweezers are fine for eyebrows and removing the stray hair here and there, but they're way too impractical and uncomfortable for other uses. Can you imagine trying to pluck out all your leg hairs? Neither can we.

☐ **Electrolysis/Epilation** – Both these methods use electric current and can be used on the face as well as other areas of the body. But, electrolysis, which uses an electric current to destroy the hair at its root, is a permanent method of hair removal. However, electrolysis is definitely not painless. It is also costly and requires repeated sessions to remove all the hair in an area of skin. It should only be done by a trained technician. Call your doctor or the International Guild of Professional Electrologists (800-830-3247) for a referral to a trained professional.

Epilating machines and tweezer electrolysis kits have some of the same advantages and drawbacks as electrolysis. Epilating machines do not remove hair permanently. The process is usually done in a salon. Home kits are now on the market, but girls should be trained in their use by a skilled operator.

## Special Skin Concerns For African-American Women

Treatments for pimples and acne and certain hair removal methods pose special problems for African-American skin. Here's how and why and what you can do to avoid these problems and care for your beautiful skin.

*Abrasive Soaps and Scrubs:* Never let them near your pretty face! They won't clear up your acne, and they may discolor dark complexions, causing patches of permanently lightened or darkened skin.

*Keloid Problems:* African-American skin is prone to abnormal formations of scar tissue known as keloids. Scar tissue is formed as part of the healing process, following a cut or other damage to the skin. But in people subject to keloid, scar tissue continues to form even after the injury is healed, resulting in an excess build-up of scar tissue. Even the seemingly minor damage to the skin caused by simply "popping" a pimple can result in an unsightly scar in a person subject to keloid formation.

*In-Grown Hairs:* Because of the curl pattern and texture their pubic hair, African-American who shave their "bikini hair" are more susceptible to developing ingrown pubic hairs which result in unsightly, irritated bumps on the skin. If this occurs, free the end of the hair from the skin, but don't don't pluck the hair itself from the skin. Because ingrown

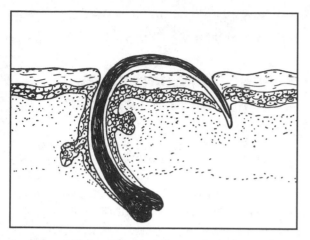

*In-Grown Hairs: The tip of a curly hair can loop back, pierce the skin's surface, and grow inward. Shaving cuts hair to a sharp tip and increases the likelihood of developing ingrown hairs.*

hairs could lead to scarring, girls who have problems with keloid should not shave this area of the body.

*Cream Hair Removers:* Because of the curl pattern and thickness of their pubic hair, African-American women may have problems using cream hair removers. In order to remove the hair, the creams have to be left on longer, increasing the chemical irritation to the skin. So always test a small patch of skin before using the cream. Use cream removers with moisturizers and natural herbs and oils (aloe, yarrow, rosemary, sage). Stay out of the sun, chlorine, and saltwater for twenty-four hours.

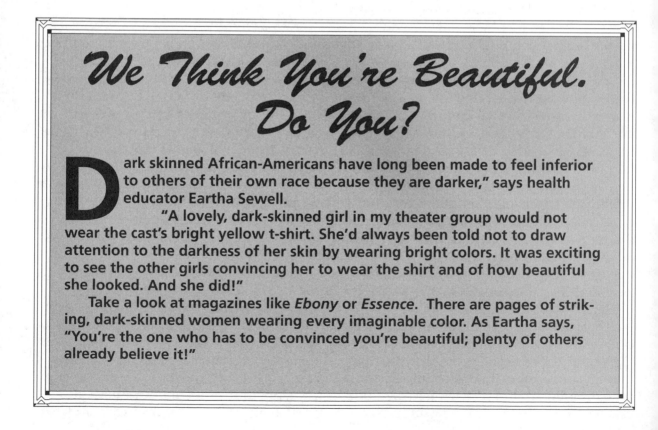

# We Think You're Beautiful. Do You?

D ark skinned African-Americans have long been made to feel inferior to others of their own race because they are darker," says health educator Eartha Sewell.

"A lovely, dark-skinned girl in my theater group would not wear the cast's bright yellow t-shirt. She'd always been told not to draw attention to the darkness of her skin by wearing bright colors. It was exciting to see the other girls convincing her to wear the shirt and of how beautiful she looked. And she did!"

Take a look at magazines like *Ebony* or *Essence*. There are pages of striking, dark-skinned women wearing every imaginable color. As Eartha says, "You're the one who has to be convinced you're beautiful; plenty of others already believe it!"

# Test Your

## with This

### (Puberty Quiz)

**True  False**

_____ _____ **1.** If you have pimples during puberty, you'll probably have them all your life.

_____ _____ **2.** Being nervous or excited can cause our perspiration and oil glands to become more active, which in turn may cause more perspiration and pimples.

_____ _____ **3.** Some girls tend to "break out" in pimples around the time of their menstrual periods.

_____ _____ **4.** Boys are more apt to have pimples during puberty than girls.

_____ _____ **5.** Blackheads are caused by little pieces of dirt under the skin.

_____ _____ **6.** A good way of getting rid of pimples is to squeeze or pop them.

_____ _____ **7.** Acne occurs when clogged pores and pimples become inflamed or infected.

_____ _____ **8.** There is no medical treatment for severe acne.

_____ _____ **9.** Eating chocolate or greasy foods causes pimples and acne.

Now turn the page to see how you did.

# ANSWERS

**1. False.** Although some people have skin problems all their lives, most of us tend to "outgrow" our pimples by the time we reach our late teens or early twenties.

**2. True.** Nervousness, excitement, or stress can cause an increase in perspiration and pimples.

**3. True.** Some girls (and women too!) tend to break out in pimples in the week or so before their periods or while they are actually menstruating.

**4. True.** Boys usually have more trouble with pimples than girls during puberty.

**5. False.** Blackheads happen because the oils that clog the skin pores turn black when they come in contact with the oxygen in the air around us. Blackheads are not caused by dirt particles under the skin.

**6. False.** Popping or squeezing pimples can leave permanent scars or pits on your skin.

**7. True.** Acne is the commonly used term for pimples that have become inflamed and/or infected.

**8. False.** Although severe acne isn't 100% curable, the condition can be successfully treated by a skilled dermatologist (skin doctor).

**9. False.** The most recent studies show that eating chocolate and greasy foods does not increase your chances of developing pimples or acne.

# Growing Up: What's In It For You?

Talking about things like B.O. and zits can make puberty sound like the pits. So, we'd like you to remind yourself of all the good things about growing up. Use the space below to make a list of the good things about growing up—things you can do now that you're not a "kid" anymore or things that you'll be able to do once you're older. Then turn the page and see how your answers compare to other girls and boys your age.

_____

_____

_____

_____

_____

_____

_____

_____

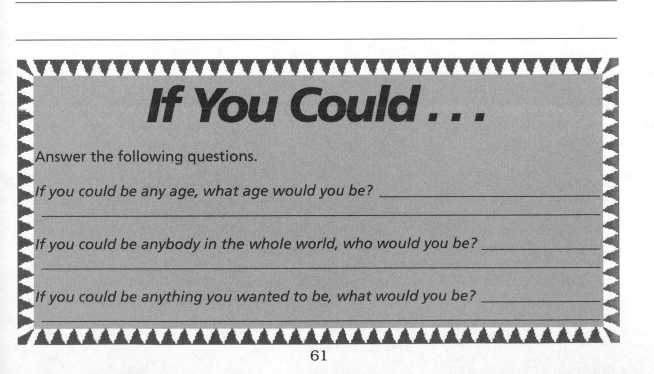

# If You Could . . .

Answer the following questions.

If you could be any age, what age would you be? _____

If you could be anybody in the whole world, who would you be? _____

If you could be anything you wanted to be, what would you be? _____

Here are some lists from other kids your age.

- More privileges
- Getting my braces off
- Getting a job
- Getting to stay out later
- Dating
- Being more my own boss
- Driving a car
- Getting into R-rated movies
- New friends
- Having my body get stronger
- Going to parties

- Knowing my old friends for a long time
- New school
- Having my own money
- More respect
- Joining the team in high school
- More allowance
- Making my own decisions (sometimes)
- Going to college
- Hanging out more with my friends
- Babysitting younger kids
- Getting really good at something (karate, art)

# PICTURE YOUR FUTURE

You've found a magic lamp, rubbed it, and out pops a genie who grants you a wish for the future. Complete the picture below by drawing a wish you have for your future.

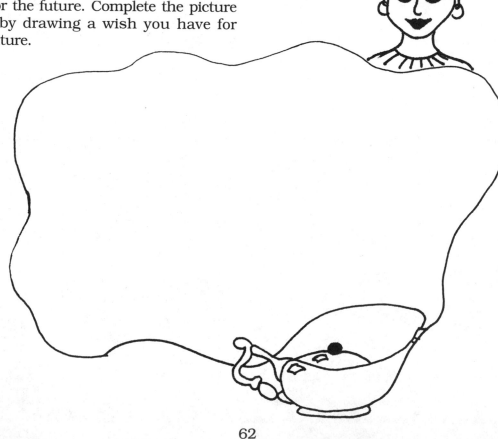

# PART FIVE

# The Female Sex Organs: An Owner's Manual

**H**uman beings are either male or female, depending on what type of sex organs they have. The female sex organs are also known as the reproductive organs because they are the parts of our bodies that make us able to reproduce—that is, to have a baby. These organs are also called the genital organs because they enable us to regenerate (a word which also refers to making babies).

We have sex, or reproductive, organs on both the inside and the outside of our bodies. External means "outside" and internal means "inside," so the sex organs on the inside are called the internal sex, reproductive, or genital organs, and those on the outside are called the external sex, reproductive, or genital organs. And just in case you aren't confused enough, the external sex organs on a female are also called the vulva.

In this section, you'll learn about the external and internal sex organs—what they look like, how they work, and how they change during puberty.

# The Vulva

The sex organs on the outside of the female body are called the vulva. The drawing below shows how the different parts of the vulva look in a grown woman.

Doing the coloring exercise below will help you to identify and to better remember the names of the various parts of the vulva. These are important parts of the body, so it's worth the effort.

## COLORING EXERCISE

Read the following descriptions of the different parts of the vulva. Locate each part on the drawing and color it according to the directions given below. (If this book isn't yours to color in, make a tracing or photocopy of the drawing and color on it.)

P.S. The directions say to use a red and a blue pencil, but any two colors will do.

MONS – A pad of fat tissue over the pubic bone. Pubic hair covers the mons in a grown woman. Color it with red polka dots.

OUTER LIPS – Two flaps or folds of skin that cover and protect the other parts of the vulva. Color them with blue polka dots.

INNER LIPS – Two more flaps or folds of skin, located inside the outer lips, that pro-

vide still more protection. Color them with blue stripes.

CLITORIS – This bud-shaped organ is the part of the vulva that's the most sensitive to touching and sexual feelings. Color the clitoris red.

URINARY OPENING – The opening through which urine ("pee") leaves the body. Circle it with blue.

VAGINAL OPENING – The opening to the vagina, the passageway that leads to the reproductive organs inside the body. Circle it with red.

ANUS – The opening through which feces (bowel movements) leave the body. This isn't really part of the vulva, and we won't color it in, but since it's in this area of the body, we wanted to mention it.

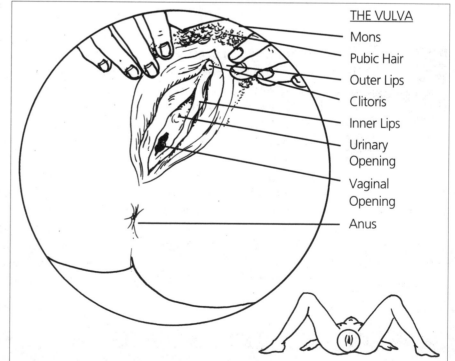

THE VULVA
- Mons
- Pubic Hair
- Outer Lips
- Clitoris
- Inner Lips
- Urinary Opening
- Vaginal Opening
- Anus

# Mirror, Mirror on the Wall...

*(Actually, a hand-held mirror will be a lot less awkward for this exercise.)*

Unlike boys, who can easily see their genitals, we need a mirror to get a really good look at ours. Using a hand-held mirror and comparing your own body to a medical illustration is the easiest, most effective way of learning about the various parts of the vulva.

Don't expect to look exactly like the drawings in this book, though. (For one thing, you won't have stripes and polka dots.) Each of us is unique and different. Also, the vulva changes as we mature, and a mature woman's vulva looks quite different than it did when she was a young girl. Nonetheless, if you can identify your own facial features (nose, mouth, eyes) from a drawing as simple as this, you can certainly learn to recognize the various parts of the vulva using the drawings in this book. In fact, with a little practice, the features of your vulva will be as plain as the nose on your face!

## A Guided Tour of Your Own Body

Grab a mirror and follow along as we take you on a guided tour of the vulva. Of course, the appearance of your vulva will depend on whether you're just starting puberty or are already well into the process. But, as we guide you on your tour, we'll explain what the different parts of the vulva look like before, during, and after puberty. So, find a quiet, private spot and perhaps some pillows to prop up your back, so you're comfortable. Bend your knees, position the mirror so that you have a good, clear view of your vulva, and you're ready to start your tour.

**The Mons:** As you look down your body from this position you'll see the soft bulge of the mons.

*Pre-puberty* – There may not be much of a bulge yet.

*Puberty/adulthood* – The fatty pad gets thicker, making more of a bulge. Pubic hairs grow on the mons.

**The Outer Lips:** As you move down along the mons, you'll see that, at the bottom, it divides into the two outer lips. Girls often notice their first pubic hairs growing along the edge of these folds of fatty tissue.

*Pre-puberty* – The lips are generally smooth and are often separated, so that their edges may not touch.

*Puberty/adulthood* – The lips get fleshier, more wrinkly, and their edges may begin to touch. Oil glands on the underside of the lips become active and may appear as small, light-colored, slightly raised bumps in the skin.

**The Inner Lips:** Spread the outer lips apart, and you'll see the inner lips, which may be smaller, larger, or about the same size as the outer lips. In fact, the inner lips may not be the same size as one another. Color and texture vary too—from light pink to black and from fairly smooth to very wrinkled.

*Pre-puberty* – The inner lips are smooth, flat, and not very distinct or noticeable.

*Puberty/adulthood* – The inner lips become fleshier, more wrinkly, and are definitely noticeable. Oil glands become active, making the tissues more moist and the color of these tissues darkens.

**The Clitoris:** If you follow the inner lips up to the top, to the point where they meet, you'll find the tip of the clitoris, the most sexually sensitive part of the vulva. It may be partly or totally covered by a fold of skin called the clitoral hood. You may need to pull back the hood in order to see the tip of the clitoris. The rest of the clitoris can't be seen because it lies beneath the surface of the skin. But, if you press firmly on the mons directly above the clitoris, you can feel the rubbery, firm, but moveable cord that is the shaft of the clitoris.

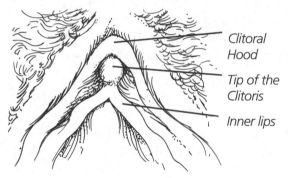

Clitoral
Hood

Tip of the
Clitoris

Inner lips

THE CLITORIS

The clitoris is very sensitive and has many nerve endings that connect to pleasure centers in our brain. Touching yourself in this area is likely to give you tingly, exciting, and pleasurable feelings (see box).

*Pre-puberty* – The clitoris is small and difficult to see.

*Puberty/adulthood* – The clitoris is larger and more sensitive. In adult women, it is about the size of an eraser on the tip of a pencil.

**The Urinary Opening:** This is the opening through which urine (pee) leaves the body. It looks like an upside down V. It can be very difficult to find, but if you move down from the clitoris in a straight line, it's the first dimpled area you come to.

*Pre-puberty* – The urinary opening is very tiny and hard to see.

*Puberty/adulthood* – The urinary opening enlarges and is more noticeable.

# Masturbation

asturbation is rubbing or touching the genitals in a way that feels good. It may lead to a wonderful, shivery, hard-to-describe feeling called orgasm. Both males and females masturbate and experience an orgasm. You may have heard that masturbation will make you blind, grow hair on your palms, or turn you into a "sex maniac." None of these things are true. There's just no way masturbation can harm you! Some people have religious or moral objections or don't feel comfortable doing it, but most people—young and old, married or not—do masturbate. It's normal if you do and normal if you don't!

The vagina is the passageway between the vulva and the sex organs inside the body. It is a short muscular tube. It is very elastic and can expand to many times it's size (big enough for a baby to pass through during childbirth). Most of the time, though, the vagina is like a collapsed balloon, with its inner walls folded up against and touching each other. The puckered folds or little bulges of flesh you see when you look at your vaginal opening are these folded-up inner walls of the vagina.

**The Vaginal Opening & Hymen:** The vagina, the passageway between the vulva and the other reproductive organs, is up inside the body, so you won't be able to see the vagina itself. But, if you move in a straight line down from the clitoris and urinary opening, you'll come to the opening of the vagina. Medical drawings usually show this opening as a gaping black hole. But, you won't see a black hole. Instead, you'll see bulges and folds of flesh which may have a sort of puckered look (see the box at the top of the page).

You may also see your hymen—a thin skin membrane just inside the vaginal opening that stretches across the opening and has one or more openings which allow for the passage of the menstrual flow during your period. As the drawing above shows, the hymen looks different in different girls. It may be just a thin fringe of tissue around the edges of the vaginal opening, or it may stretch partly or completely across the vaginal opening and have one large or several small openings.

*Pre-puberty* – The vaginal opening is small. The hymen is thin and not very distinct.

*Puberty* – The hymen gets thicker and is easier to see, though many girls still have difficulty locating the hymen because it's inside the vaginal opening. Only rarely is a girl born without a hymen. However, it is possible for a girl to tear or stretch her hymen during an accidental fall or vigorous exercise (gymnastics, horseback riding).

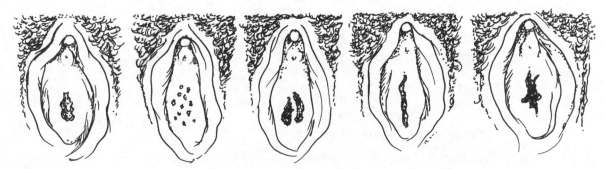

*These are just some of the many ways the hymen may look.*

67

## There's Another Name For It

Use the space below to make a quick list of other names you've heard for the vulva or for any of its various parts.

Your list can include scientific or medical terms, baby words, and slang words, even so-called "dirty" words (after all, this is your own private book).

_____

_____

_____

_____

## *You're No Dumb Elbow!*

Chances are, nobody's ever called you a dumb elbow, and we doubt that you've ever lost your temper and called someone a stupid foot. But, take a look at the list you just made and then think of all the names—both the proper and improper ones—for the male sex organs. Then think

of the insults and bouts of name-calling you've heard. We bet you've heard the names for the sexual parts of the body used to insult someone.

You never hear people called dumb elbows or stupid feet, but you do hear dumb or stupid or some other put-down along with the name of a sex organ? Why is that? Use the space below to jot down your ideas about this. Then put the question to your friends and family and compare their answers to yours.

_____

_____

_____

_____

_____

_____

_____

## You Said It!

**In talking about the sex organs on the outside of your body, we've used some words that may be new to you. This will help you learn to pronounce these words correctly.**

**Clitoris (KLIT-or-iss)**      **Genitals (JEN-uh-tuhls)**      **Hymen (HI-muhn)**
**Mons (MONZ)**      **Pubic (PEW-bik)**      **Urinary (YOUR-in-air-ee)**
                     **Vulva (VUL-vuh)**

**If you're still not certain how to pronounce any of these words, check it out with your mom, your dad, or another adult you trust.**

# Test Your

# I.Q.

## with This

# P.Q.

## (Puberty Quiz)

| True | False | | |
|------|-------|---|---|
| ____ | ____ | **1.** | During puberty, the inner and outer lips get fleshier and darker in color. |
| ____ | ____ | **2.** | The outer lips and the hymen may not be very noticeable before puberty. |
| ____ | ____ | **3.** | Once a person gets married, he or she stops masturbating. |
| ____ | ____ | **4.** | During puberty, oil glands on the inner and outer lips become more active, giving the vulva a feeling of "wetness." |
| ____ | ____ | **5.** | When a female is masturbating or when she has "sexy" thoughts or feelings, her vaginal area may become lubricated with a clear liquid. |
| ____ | ____ | **6.** | About a year or two before her period starts, a girl may notice a clear to milky white discharge from her vaginal opening that may leave a slightly yellowish stain on her underwear. |
| ____ | ____ | **7.** | The inner lips are approximately the same size and are always smaller than the outer lips. |

# ANSWERS

· · · · · · · · · · · · · · · · · · · · · · · · · · · · · · · · · · · · · · · · · · · ·

**1. True.** These are all normal puberty changes.

**2. True.** During puberty, the outer lips and hymen become larger and more noticeable.

**3. False.** Many married people masturbate—either alone or with their husbands or wives.

**4. True.** The oil glands in the vulva—and sweat glands too—become more active during puberty and contribute to a new feeling of wetness in the vulva.

**5. True.** Oil and mucous glands in the vulva and vagina respond to sexual stimulation by producing fluids that lubricate the vagina. Vaginal discharge also contributes to this feeling of wetness.

**6. True.** These vaginal discharges are perfectly normal, another sign that your body is maturing.

**7. False.** The inner lips are not always the same size and they may be larger and protrude further than the outer lips.

## The Internal Reproductive Organs

Now that you're familiar with the sex organs on the outside of your body, let's take a look at the ones on the inside of your body. The drawing below shows the internal female reproductive organs.

Read the descriptions of the various organs below. Then grab your colored pencils and color each organ according to the directions given below. (If this book isn't yours to color in, make a tracing or photocopy of the drawing to color on.)

P.S. The directions say to use a red and a blue pencil, but any two colors will do.

**OVARIES** – Two rounded organs, one on either side of the uterus, that contain the ova, the female reproductive cells. Color the ovaries with red and blue polka dots.

**UTERINE TUBES** – Two hollow tubes connected to the upper uterus on either side. Ova travel through the tube on their way to the uterus. Color the tubes blue.

**UTERUS** – A hollow organ with thick muscular walls which are highly elastic and can stretch to many times their normal size during pregnancy as the baby grows. Draw a red circle around the uterus.

**UTERINE LINING** – The bloody tissue lining of the uterus that thickens and is shed during the monthly menstrual period if pregnancy does not occur. Color it red.

**CERVIX** – The lower part of the uterus that protrudes into the top of the vagina and has a tiny tunnel in it's center that is the passageway between the uterus and the vagina. Color the cervix blue.

**VAGINA** – The muscular tube that is the passageway between the uterus and the vulva. Color the vagina red.

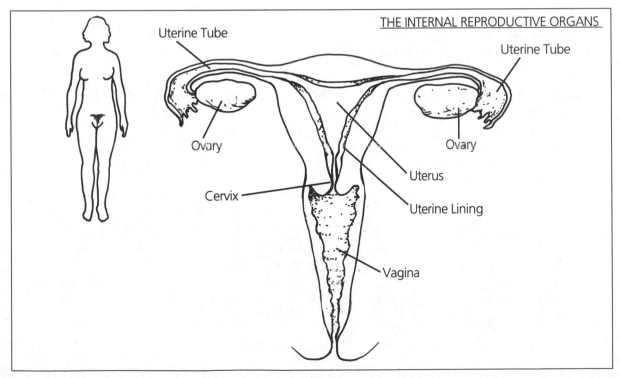

THE INTERNAL REPRODUCTIVE ORGANS

Uterine Tube

Uterine Tube

Ovary

Ovary

Uterus

Cervix

Uterine Lining

Vagina

# The Internal Growth Spurt

You get taller, your feet get bigger—it's all part of the puberty growth spurt. But, it's not just your bones that go through a growth spurt. Your reproductive organs are also affected and undergo a period of rapid growth, reaching nearly their adult size. Check out the drawings on the facing page, and you'll see what we mean.

## CHANGING SIZE AND SHAPE

Just as the proportions of your body and face change during the puberty growth spurt, so the proportions of certain internal organs change. For example, the uterus, including the cervix, grows. As it grows, the uterus also changes shape. In a child, the uterus is tube-shaped. In an adult woman, the uterus is about the size and shape of an upside-down pear.

## CHANGING POSITION

The two drawings below are side views of the female pelvic cavity. The first shows

*For purposes of comparison, these uteri are shown without their uterine tubes. The body of the uterus is the portion above the dotted line; the shaded portion below the line is the cervix.*

**Childhood**     **Puberty**     **Adulthood**

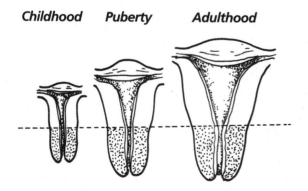

the internal reproductive organs in a young girl. The second shows the same organs in a grown woman.

In addition to increasing in size and changing proportions during puberty, the uterus also changes position. Before

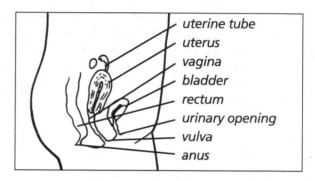

*Side view, young girl*

*Side view, woman*

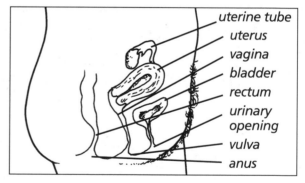

puberty, it is nearly vertical (straight up and down). But, during puberty, the back wall of the vagina grows more than its front wall. Coupled with changes in the proportions of the uterus, this is enough to tilt the uterus forward so that, in most grown women, it is tilted forward, over the bladder.

## Uterus Cut-Outs

These illustrations are actual life-size drawings of the uterus in a typical eleven-year-old girl and in a grown woman. Make a photocopy or tracing of the two drawings, cut along the dotted lines, and hold them up to your own body. Ask your mom or another adult woman to "model" the adult size for you.

(If you're surprised to find how small the uterus is, remember, it may not be very big, but it's veeery elastic—so stretchable that a baby can grow in there.)

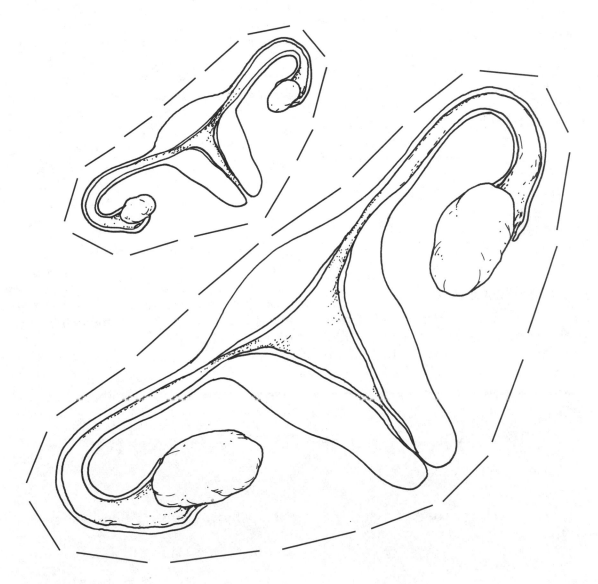

# The Female Reproductive System

Together, the internal reproductive organs comprise the female reproductive system, your body's system for making a baby. Beginning at puberty, the internal female organs go through a series of monthly changes that make it possible for you to become pregnant.

Of course, you're not ready to be a parent yet and probably won't be for some years. Even when you are ready, it's unlikely that you'll want to keep having children one right after the other. You won't be trying to get pregnant each and every month! Nonetheless, the monthly cycle of changes that prepare your body for pregnancy is repeated over and over again, month after month, throughout a woman's reproductive years, so your body will be ready if and when you do decide to have a baby.

## The Amazing Ovum

The ovum (plural, ova) is the female egg, or reproductive cell. You could think of the ovum as a set of blueprints for con-structing a human being—or, rather, half of a set of blueprints. The other half is contained in the sperm, the male reproductive cell. If an ovum is fertilized by (joined with) a male sperm, a baby can grow.

A girl is born with hundreds of thousands of ova nestled deep inside her ovaries. Each ovum is encased inside a tiny sac. As puberty begins, some of the sacs and their ova start to mature and move toward the surface of the ovary.

When a sac containing an ovum reaches the surface, it presses on the outer covering of the ovary, forming a tiny blister-like bubble. At some point during her puberty years, a girl ovulates for the first time. The bubble containing the ovum bursts open, and the ovum pops off the surface of the ovary. This process of releasing a ripe ovum from the ovary is called ovulation.

At first, a girl doesn't ovulate regularly. But, a grown woman usually ovulates about once a month throughout her reproductive years, unless she's pregnant (in which case ovulation stops until after the baby is born).

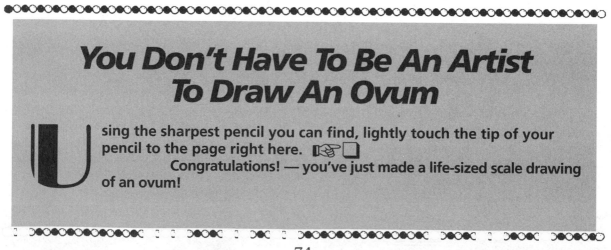

## You Don't Have To Be An Artist To Draw An Ovum

Using the sharpest pencil you can find, lightly touch the tip of your pencil to the page right here. ☞ ☐
Congratulations! — you've just made a life-sized scale drawing of an ovum!

## Ovulation & The Ovum's Journey Through the Tube

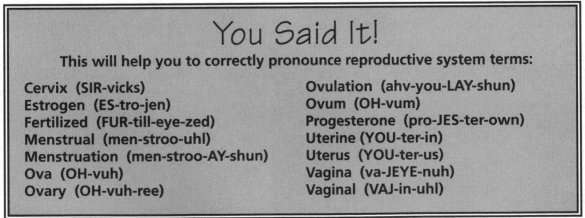

Ovum
Bubble
Ovary

About a month after she ovulates, a woman ovulates again. Another group of ova begin to ripen and move toward the surface of the ovary. The ovum to be released this month presses on the ovary's outer covering, forming the blister-like bubble which bursts as ovulation occurs again.

At the same time that the new group of ova begin moving toward the surface of the ovary in preparation for ovulation, the bloody tissue lining of the uterus has begun to grow thicker. New blood vessels form, along with spongy tissues to cushion them, and the lining grows rich in nutrients. By the time ovulation occurs, the uterine lining has doubled in thickness. The uterine lining is preparing itself because, if the ovum is fertilized and pregnancy occurs, the thick, rich lining will cushion and nourish the developing pregnancy.

It's thought that the ovaries take turns ovulating—one month it's the right ovary that releases an ovum; the next month, it's the left ovary. After the ovum has popped off the ovary, the fringed ends of the uterine tube on that side reach out like tiny fingers to grasp the ovum and draw it into the tube. Tiny muscles in the tube tighten and relax rhythmically, causing the tiny hairs that line the inside of the tube to sway back and forth, creating a stir that sweeps the ovum along the length of the tube. It takes about four days for the ovum to travel the four-inch length of the tube.

At this point, one of two things may happen—to find out what, turn to pages 76 and 78.

---

## You Said It!

**This will help you to correctly pronounce reproductive system terms:**

**Cervix (SIR-vicks)**
**Estrogen (ES-tro-jen)**
**Fertilized (FUR-till-eye-zed)**
**Menstrual (men-stroo-uhl)**
**Menstruation (men-stroo-AY-shun)**
**Ova (OH-vuh)**
**Ovary (OH-vuh-ree)**

**Ovulation (ahv-you-LAY-shun)**
**Ovum (OH-vum)**
**Progesterone (pro-JES-ter-own)**
**Uterine (YOU-ter-in)**
**Uterus (YOU-ter-us)**
**Vagina (va-JEYE-nuh)**
**Vaginal (VAJ-in-uhl)**

# Pregnancy:

**I**f the ovum has been fertilized, the woman can become pregnant. The fertilized ovum arrives in the uterus about five to seven days after ovulation. For the first few days, it floats freely in the hollow of the uterus. Then (on about the eighth day after ovulation), the fertilized ovum implants in the rich lining on one of the inside walls of the uterus, and over the next nine months, grows into a baby.

## Pregnancy and Childbirth

Pregnancy lasts about nine months, and during that time the fertilized ovum that is implanted on the inside wall of the uterus develops to the point where the baby is ready to be born.

When the time for birth is near, the mother feels the muscles of her uterus firmly contracting every few minutes. As the squeezing gets stronger, the cervix (the opening at the bottom of the uterus) gradually stretches open more and more. This may take many hours. Finally the cervix stretches open wide enough for the baby's head to pass through. Then the contracting of her uterus and the mother's efforts to bear down push the baby into the vagina, usually head first. (The vagina and vaginal opening, like the uterus and cervix, are very elastic.)

2 months   5 months   6 months   8 months   9 months

Then, usually within minutes, the baby's head, shoulders, and finally the rest of its body emerge into the world.

When a baby comes out, it is still attached to the umbilical cord. During pregnancy the cord supplied nourishment and oxygen from the mother to the baby. Because it is no longer needed, the cord is painlessly cut. Your belly button marks the point where the cord was once attached to your body.

Childbirth: The cervix opens up, allowing the baby to leave the uterus and pass into the vagina. The elastic vagina and it's opening stretch as the baby passes through on its way out into the world.

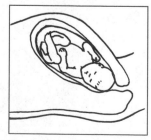
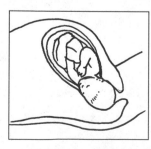
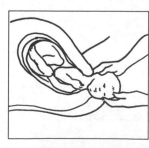
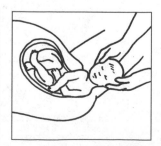

## What Happened on Your Birth Day?

We don't mean the day you eat ice cream and cake and celebrate being another year older. That's your birthday. We're talking about your birth day—the day you were born!

Get ready to do an interview. Depending on your family situation, you might interview one or both of your "natural" adoptive, or foster parents, your grandparents, or whatever adult(s) you live. We've listed some sample questions. Adapt them to suit your family situation. For instance, if your adoptive parents weren't at your birth, you can ask about when they first saw you. And, add some questions of your own.

### Sample Questions

**1.** Where was I born? (city, hospital, etc.) At what time was I born?

**2.** Did I take a long time to come or was I born quickly?

**3.** What was the weather like on the day I was born?

**4.** Who else was there that day? (family, friends, medical persons, etc.)

**5.** How much did I weigh? How many inches long was I?

**6.** What did I look like?

**7.** How was my name chosen?

**8.** Did anything unusual or funny happen when I was born?

**9.** Can you tell me what else you remember about the day I was born.?

The most interesting thing I learned about my birth day was:

_____

_____

_____

_____

_____

_____

## EXTRA, EXTRA, Read All About It!

Now that you have an idea of what happened in your world on your birth day, what about the rest of the world? Your arrival was undoubtedly the biggest thing that happened to your parents that day. But, you probably didn't make the front page of the paper. Who did? What was the headline story in the paper on your birth day?

A trip to the library will answer your question. Ask the librarian to help you find out the headline news on the day you were born. You can look at local, regional, and national newspapers in the library's collection of back issues. You might ask if *Time, Newsweek, Rolling Stone,* or any other magazine had an issue that came out the same day you did.

Make a birthday present for yourself. Photocopy one of the front pages or magazine covers published on your birth day and frame it!

# Pregnancy

**I**f the ovum is not fertilized, pregnancy does not occur. The ovum does not implant itself in the uterus, but instead disintegrates after a few days. The uterine lining which has grown rich and thick in preparation for a possible pregnancy is not needed; thus, it breaks down and is shed during the menstrual period.

## Menstruation

Most of the time the woman's ovum is not fertilized and she does not become pregnant. So, about two weeks after ovulation, the newly grown portion of the uterine lining begins to break down. The tissues of the lining disintegrate, and pieces of the lining slide off the walls of the uterus. The blood and watery tissue from the lining collect in the bottom of the uterus. This collection of blood and tissue is known as the menstrual flow, menstrual blood, or menstrual discharge.

The tiny cervical canal that runs through the center of the cervix opens up ever so slightly, allowing the collected blood and tissue to leave the uterus. The menstrual discharge dribbles through the cervical canal, down the vaginal walls, and out the vaginal opening. It doesn't come out all at once, but over a period of several days. The bleeding continues until all the newly grown lining is shed. This may take anywhere from two to eight days, but in adult women, the bleeding typically lasts about five days. Altogether, only about $\frac{1}{4}$–$\frac{3}{4}$ of a cup of blood dribbles out of the vaginal opening over this two-to eight-day period (though it often seems like more than this).

This breaking down and shedding of the uterine lining is called menstruation,

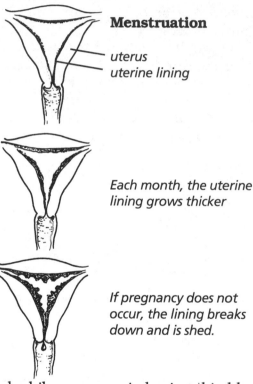

**Menstruation**

uterus
uterine lining

Each month, the uterine lining grows thicker

If pregnancy does not occur, the lining breaks down and is shed.

and while a woman is having this bloody discharge, we say she is menstruating, or "having her period."

Grown women generally have a menstrual period about once a month, but young women who have just started menstruating may have theirs more or less often than this. We'll talk more about menstruation and what you can expect from your period in the next several pages. And we'll also tell you a bit about the hormones that control menstruation.

# The Menstrual Cycle

Shortly after the uterine lining has been shed and the menstrual period is over, the uterus begins growing a new lining. Meanwhile, back in the woman's ovary, more ova are ripening inside their sacs and are moving toward the surface of the ovary. One of these sacs will reach the surface and press against the outer covering of the ovary, forming a tiny bubble. The bubble will burst, and once again, a ripe ovum will be released from the ovary. If that ovum is not fertilized, the newly grown lining will again break down and be shed from the uterus, and the woman will have another menstrual period.

This cycle of menstruation and ovulation, which is repeated over and over again during a woman's reproductive years, is called the menstrual cycle. Each time a woman has her period, a new cycle begins, and the first day of bleeding during the menstrual period is called Day 1 of the cycle. In grown women, one complete cycle—that is, the entire process of menstruation and ovulation, counting from Day 1 of one cycle to Day 1 of the next—

normally takes anywhere from twenty-one to thirty-six days, with the average cycle being twenty-eight-days long. However, few women have their periods like clockwork, exactly every twenty-eight days, year in and year out. For most of us there is at least some variation in the length of the cycle from time to time.

Young women—teens who have only been menstruating for a couple of years—are especially likely to have periods that come at irregular intervals. It typically takes one to three years for a girl to establish a regular pattern of menstruating. A girl may have may have her first period and not have her next one for two months or six months or even longer. Or her first period may be followed by a second period three weeks later. Even when young women's periods do become fairly regular and predictable, the range of cycle lengths is greater among young women in their teens and early twenties than it is among older women. It's normal for young women to have a cycle length between twenty-one to forty-four days, as opposed to the typical cycle of twenty-one to thirty-six days in grown women.

## Can You Unscramble This Cycle?

Here are the major events of the menstrual cycle, but the order is scrambled. See if you can put the events listed in the first column in their proper order by writing them in the space provided in the second column. The cycle begins and ends with menstruation, so we've filled those in for you. When you're finished, compare your answers to the illustration on the next page.

Menstruation-Lining Shed; Ova Maturing

| | |
|---|---|
| **Ovum Reaches Uterus and Dissolves** | _____ |
| **Ovum Matures; Lining Thickens** | _____ |
| **Ovum Moves Through Tube** | _____ |
| **Lining Breaks Down** | _____ |
| **Ovulation-Ovum Released** | _____ |

Menstruation-Lining Shed; Ova Maturing

79

# The Typical Twenty-eight-day Cycle

You could think of the menstrual cycle as a filmstrip or movie that runs continuously, over and over again, back to back without interruption. The illustration above shows what happens over the course of a typical twenty-eight-day menstrual cycle.

**Days 1–5:** During the first five days, the uterine lining is being shed and the woman is having her period. At the same time, a new group of ova is beginning to develop inside the ovary.

**Days 6–13:** During days 6–13, the ova are maturing inside their sacs and moving toward the surface of the ovary. At the same time, the uterine lining is growing thick and rich in nutrients in preparation for a possible pregnancy.

**Day 14:** By Day 14 of the typical twenty-eight-day cycle, the uterine lining is twice as thick as it was at the end of the bleeding on Day 5. And, on Day 14 of the typical twenty-eight-day cycle, ovulation occurs.

**Days 14–19:** For the next four to five days the ovum is traveling through the uterine tube toward the uterus. The uterine lining is growing still thicker.

**Days 20–28:** The ovum reaches the uterus. If pregnancy does not occur, the ovum dissolves, usually by Day 20. Beginning on Day 21, the uterine lining starts to deteriorate. This breaking down of the lining continues through Day 28. Then the uterus begins to shed the blood and watery tissues of the disintegrated lining. This is the first day of menstrual bleeding and is actually Day 1 of the next menstrual cycle.

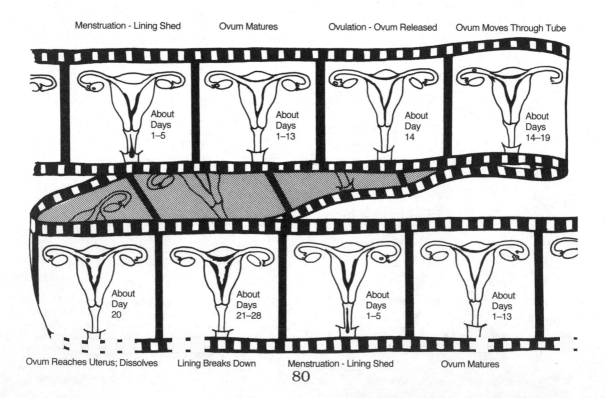

Menstruation - Lining Shed     Ovum Matures     Ovulation - Ovum Released     Ovum Moves Through Tube

About Days 1–5     About Days 1–13     About Day 14     About Days 14–19

About Day 20     About Days 21–28     About Days 1–5     About Days 1–13

Ovum Reaches Uterus; Dissolves     Lining Breaks Down     Menstruation - Lining Shed     Ovum Matures

## WHAT'S NORMAL AND WHAT'S NOT?

Are your periods coming too often?...not often enough? Does your period last too long? Are you bleeding too much?...Girls usually have lots of questions about what's normal and what's not when it comes to menstruation. If you've had questions, we think you'll find the following "Menstrual Fact Sheet" helpful.

## *Menstrual Fact Sheet*

✔ **Length of the cycle:** A cycle runs from the first day of bleeding of one period to the first day of bleeding of the next period. For adult women, cycles lasting anywhere from twenty-one to thirty-six days are normal. For younger women (teens and early twenties), normal cycles can last from twenty-one to forty-four days. Many doctors now feel a girl should be checked if she repeatedly has cycles shorter than twenty-one days or longer than forty-four days.

✔ **Number of days of bleeding:** Anywhere from two to seven days is considered normal. If your periods consistently last more than seven days, see your doctor. This usually isn't the sign of a serious problem but it should be checked out.

✔ **Amount of menstrual flow:** You may shed anywhere from 1-2 tablespoons to $1/4$ - $1/3$ of a cup of menstrual blood during your period. The amount of blood may be about the same each time or it may vary, being very heavy one month and lighter the next. Either pattern is normal.

If you're soaking through (and we mean literally soaking through) more than a pad or a tampon every hour for an entire day, your flow is too heavy. This is not normal, and you should consult your doctor.

✔ **Patterns of menstrual flow:** Some women tend to bleed most heavily on the first day or two of their periods, gradually trickling off until there is only a light flow on the last day. Others start off lightly, then get heavier. Still others will bleed for a couple of days, then stop or slow down for a day or so and start again. All of these patterns are considered normal.

Some women have pretty much the same pattern each month. Others follow one pattern for a month or two or more, then their pattern changes. This, too, is normal.

✔ **Color of the flow:** The menstrual blood may be bright red, light pink, or even brownish in color. It may be the same color each time or the color may vary from period to period or within one period.

✔ **Clots:** You may notice thick clumps of blood in your menstrual flow. These are called clots and you are more apt to notice clots in the morning when you first get up, for the blood has been pooling and congealing in the top of your vagina while you've been lying down asleep. Clots are considered normal. As long as the amount of flow is normal, clots aren't anything to worry about.

✔ **Cramps:** Cramps are pains in the lower abdomen that may occur during, or in the week or so before, your period. Mild to moderate cramps are common and completely normal. However, if your cramps are severe enough to limit your normal activities, you should see a doctor. (P.S. If you have cramps, see page 113.)

## Vaginal Discharges

Sometime in the six months to a year or so before her first period, a girl may notice a clear or milky white discharge from the vagina that sometimes leaves a yellowish stain on the underpants when it dries. This is a completely normal sign that a girl is growing up. It's called the vaginal discharge, or vaginal secretion. It is made up of secretions from the cervix and the old, dead cells shed from the vagina. Just as the skin on the surface of our bodies is constantly shedding old cells, so the skin on the vagina sheds cells. As we go through puberty, this shedding speeds up. The cervix makes fluids and mucus to wash away these cells and cleanse the vagina. This is what causes the discharge and yellowish stain. The discharge may be heavier on some days than on others.

Once a girl begins to menstruate, she may notice even more of this discharge, especially at certain times of the month. On the days right after her period, a female usually doesn't have too much discharge, and her vagina and vaginal lips are apt to feel rather dry. After a few days, the glands in the cervix make more fluid and mucus, and the vagina and vaginal lips are "wetter." The discharge on these days is often clear to white to slightly yellowish in color and may be thin and watery or thick, pasty, and sticky.

Around the time of month when your ovary releases its ripe ovum, the discharge tends to be clear and very slippery. If you were to put some between your fingers, it would stretch into clear slippery strands. In a few females, discharge at this time of month may be tinged red or brown, due to the bit of bleeding that some females have when they ovulate. This light staining, or "spotting," is perfectly normal. Some females don't have much discharge for the rest of their cycle, though others do.

Vaginal discharge is perfectly normal. If, however, it begins to have a foul smell, to cause itching or redness, to have a greenish color, or to have tiny bubbles or small chunks (like cottage cheese) in it, this may be the sign of a vaginal infection. Although vaginal infections are not usually serious, you should see a doctor and have the infection treated so it will clear up and won't get worse.

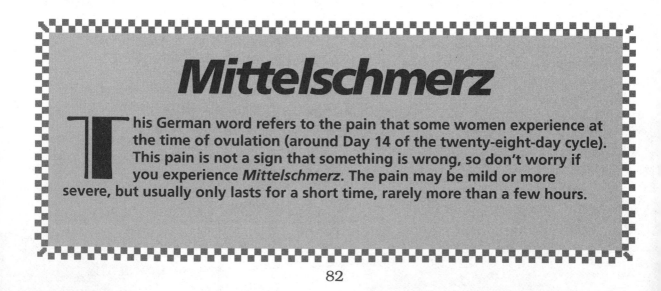

# Mittelschmerz

This German word refers to the pain that some women experience at the time of ovulation (around Day 14 of the twenty-eight-day cycle). This pain is not a sign that something is wrong, so don't worry if you experience *Mittelschmerz*. The pain may be mild or more severe, but usually only lasts for a short time, rarely more than a few hours.

# Hormones

Hormones regulate a woman's monthly cycle of ovulation and menstruation. They're responsible for breast development, pubic hair, the growth spurt, pimples, perspiration, the fat pads that grow on your hips, and just about all the other changes that take place in your body during puberty. In fact, they're what causes puberty to happen in the first place.

But what are they?

Hormones are chemicals made in one part of the body that travel through the bloodstream to other parts of the body and cause these other organs to develop or behave in a certain way. You could think of hormones as a sort of chemical messenger system.

The body makes many different hormones. You could go crazy just trying to remember all their names. But the illustration below will give you an idea of how hormones work, mentioning only the hormones that are especially important in menstruation and puberty.

*Puberty starts in the head. Around the age of eight or nine, a girl begins to produce a certain hormone at the base of the brain. Gradually, the amount of hormone made by the brain increases and a girl's hormone levels rise.*

*The hormones from the brain travel through the bloodstream to the ovaries and cause some of the sacs that contain the ova to move toward the surface of the ovary and to make a hormone of their own called estrogen.*

*Estrogen travels throughout the body, and is responsible for many of the changes that take place during puberty, including a girl's first menstrual period. Estrogen, along with a second ovarian hormone called progesterone and other hormones, controls the menstrual cycle—the cycle of ovulation followed by menstruation that is repeated, over and over again, throughout a woman's reproductive years.*

# Invent Your Own Puberty Rite

For the most part, puberty rites have disappeared from modern society, but throughout much of human history, in culture after culture, a girl's first menstrual period and her entrance into womanhood was accompanied by rituals, ceremonies, and customs known as puberty rites. Some of these puberty rites grew out of primitive, fearful beliefs about menstruation and were pretty horrible. But there have also been puberty rites involving feasting and celebrations, including one from India which ends with the girl sitting on a throne, while her family and neighbors come by and lay gifts at her feet!

It's unlikely that you'll be able sell your family and neighbors on the gifts-at-your-feet routine, but why not invent a puberty rite of your own?

A modern puberty rite could take many forms—a special moonlight ceremony, a slumber party with all your female relatives, a special gift to pass on to the next generation...it could be anything. In one family we know, the father promised to take the daughter on a special trip of her choosing, and when the big day came, off they went to Las Vegas!

We started a puberty rite that we hope will become a family tradition. We decided that when Area got her first period she would receive an opal ring of Lynda's. Actually, we got so excited about some of the other puberty changes, that Area got the ring a bit early. She got a second opal ring when her period started, and she's saving them both for a day when she has a daughter going through puberty.

Invent your own puberty rite. Use the space below to describe your idea.

_____

_____

_____

Now, cover your answer and ask your parent(s) to invent a puberty rite. Have them use the space below to describe their ideas.

_____

_____

Read each other's answers. Compare and discuss your ideas and agree on a puberty rite for your family. Describe your plans in the space below.

_____

_____

# 6 THE BIG M

T his part of the book is a nitty, gritty, practical guide to menstruation. These pages will also help you to examine your own and other people's attitudes and feelings about menstruation.

Throughout history, menstruation has had a bad reputation. In Biblical times, a menstruating woman was "unclean," and had to atone each month for her "sin" ("her unclean discharge") with the sacrifice of two turtledoves and pigeons.

In ancient Rome, menstrual blood wasn't merely unclean, it was deadly! According to the leading science text of the day, mere contact with it could make your wine go sour, dry up the seeds in your garden, cause all the fruit to fall off your trees, kill hives of bees, cause metals to rust instantly, and fill the air with a horrible odor. And, an actual taste of the vile stuff was supposedly enough to drive dogs mad and infect their bites with an incurable poison!

In primitive societies, women were banished to "menstrual huts" each month. Getting a week's vacation every month with your girlfriends may not sound like a bad idea. But menstruation was considered a shameful thing and being sent to the huts was probably more like being sent to jail than going on vacation.

Of course, we no longer send women off to menstrual huts each month. We now know that all those old myths are just so much nonsense. In our modern, enlightened age, we no longer have those old negative attitudes toward menstruation—do we?

## "The Curse"

"The Curse" is one of the most common slang terms for menstrual periods. Do you know any others? In the space to the right, list as many as you can. Ask friends and family to add to the list.

Now, look over your list. Are most of the terms on your list negative or positive? What does this tell you about people's attitudes toward menstruation?

Make up your own slang term with a positive message about menstruation and write it here_____

## Menstrual Slang Terms

_____

_____

_____

_____

_____

_____

_____

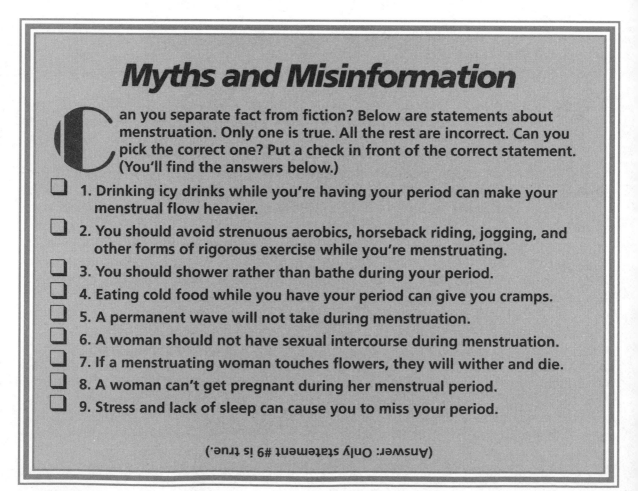

# Myths and Misinformation

**C**an you separate fact from fiction? Below are statements about menstruation. Only one is true. All the rest are incorrect. Can you pick the correct one? Put a check in front of the correct statement. (You'll find the answers below.)

☐ 1. Drinking icy drinks while you're having your period can make your menstrual flow heavier.

☐ 2. You should avoid strenuous aerobics, horseback riding, jogging, and other forms of rigorous exercise while you're menstruating.

☐ 3. You should shower rather than bathe during your period.

☐ 4. Eating cold food while you have your period can give you cramps.

☐ 5. A permanent wave will not take during menstruation.

☐ 6. A woman should not have sexual intercourse during menstruation.

☐ 7. If a menstruating woman touches flowers, they will wither and die.

☐ 8. A woman can't get pregnant during her menstrual period.

☐ 9. Stress and lack of sleep can cause you to miss your period.

(Answer: Only statement #9 is true.)

86

# First Impressions

Ready for an interview? Here's what you do—go ask at least four people (men, women, boys, or girls) the questions:

- When did you first hear about menstruation?
- What did you hear?
- How did you feel about it?

Note their answers below.

*Who I Asked*                    *Age*                              *What They Said*

_____

_____

_____

_____

_____

_____

_____

_____

_____

One thing I learned from doing this interview is:_____

_____

_____

_____

# Thoughts & Feelings: Menstruation

I'm really anxious. I have a pad hidden in my bookcase and I keep reading books, so I'm prepared. I even dreamt I got my period.

—Corinna, age 11

Just the other day I started my period. It gushed and I think it is definitely the grossest thing that has ever happened to me.

—Claire, age 13

I'm really proud because I have always been really afraid I'd be the last kid in my grade to start.

—Monica, age 11

I'm kind of nervous about having it. What if I got my period, and I had white pants on? Now that's scary!

—Gennie, age 12

# HOW DO YOU FEEL?

Complete these sentences:

The first time I got my period I felt (will feel) _____.

Periods are _____.

If I saw blood on the back of a girl's skirt or pants, I would feel _____.

The first time I found out about periods I_____

_____.

If men menstruated,_____

_____.

# How Do Your Friends Feel?

**F**or this project, you'll need to make a "book" of blank pages. Fold a piece of construction paper and a few blank pieces of paper in half. Slip the folded sheets of blank paper inside the construction paper and staple together to form your "book."

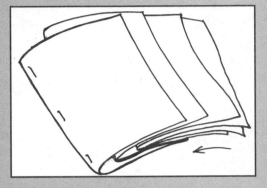

On the first page of your book write:

> *At the top of each page in this book, there's a sentence stem for you to complete. Write your ending for the sentence anywhere on the page below the sentence stem. Don't sign your name, and don't too write too large. You need to leave room for other people to write because when you've completed all the sentences, you're going to pass this book on to someone else. Tell that person to complete the sentences and then pass the book along to another person.*
>
> *If there's no more room in the book after you've written in it or if you can't find anyone to pass it to, please return the book to me.*
>
> *If you want to see the book when it's all done, just ask me.*
>
> Signed,_____
>
> Sign your name here

Now copy the first sentence stem from page 42 on the top of the first page of your book; copy the second sentence stem on the second page, and so on. Then, make up some sentence stems of your own and enter them in your book. Fill your entire book so that all of your pages have a sentence stem on the top. Now you're ready to start your book on its rounds by passing it along to a friend.

( P.S. If your book doesn't come back within a few days, you better start tracking it down!)

# HILARY'S FIRST PERIOD

Fill in the blanks in the story below.

This morning Hilary woke up and discovered that she'd begun to menstruate. She knew this because _____

_____

Hilary's mom had told her about menstruation and she'd also learned about it in her health class at school. But now that it was actually happening to her, she felt a little embarrassed about _____

_____

On the other hand, she felt good about _____

_____

_____

Even though she'd learned a lot about menstruation, Hilary found that she still had a question about _____

_____

_____

To find out the answer to her question, she decided to _____

_____

_____

Hilary is _____ years old.

Adapted from *New Methods for Puberty Education*, Grades 4-9 (which is the best puberty curriculum around). Available from Planned Parenthood of Greater New Jersey, 575 Main Street, Hackensack, NJ 07601. (Cost is $29.95 plus $3.00 shipping and handling.)

## Another Version

It might be fun for you to see how your answers compare with someone else's. Read "Hilary's First Period" aloud to your mom, another adult woman you feel close to, an older sister, or maybe your best friend. You might want to jot down notes on her answers in the space below. Then, compare your answers and hers. Explain how they were similar or different and answer the questions below.

_____

_____

_____

_____

_____

_____

_____

_____

_____

## How Old Did You Think Hilary Was?

If you wrote that Hilary was somewhere between nine and sixteen years old, you gave a good answer because 95 out of every 100 girls in this country get their first periods sometime between their ninth and sixteenth birthdays. And, if you guessed that Hilary was twelve or thirteen, you were right on the ticket. In the U.S. the "average" age for starting to menstruate is 12.8 years of age. Remember, though, few of us are exactly average and there are plenty of girls who start to menstruate when they are either younger or older than this.

## *Your First Period—When?*

No one can say for sure just when you'll get your first menstrual period, but the clues in the next several pages can help you make a pretty good "guess-timate" (a cross between a guess and an estimate). If you've already started menstruating, you may want to fill in the clues anyway, just to have a record.

# Clue #1

Girls often take after their mothers and other female relatives when it comes to menstruation. In the right hand column make a list of female relatives you could question about their periods. Your list could include your mom, and any sisters, grandmother, aunts, or cousins (on your mother's side of the family). Don't question your stepmother or adoptive mom though, only blood relatives.

Ask each woman on your list if she got her period earlier, later, or about the same time as the other girls her age. Note her answer on your list by writing "earlier," "later," or "about average" right after her name.

Then, look over your list. Can you see a family tendency, a common pattern among your relatives? Did most get their

**Your Relative**      **Her Answer**

periods earlier than their classmates?…later than the other girls?…at about the same time as most of the others, at around the average age?

Your family may not have a common pattern or particular tendency. But, if there is a common family pattern, chances are that you'll follow this same pattern.

# Hot Tip from Big Sis

There's a tendency for younger sisters to get their periods at an earlier age than their older sisters did. Exactly how much earlier depends on how many older brothers and sisters the girl has. Not all families follow this pattern. But, if yours does, filling in the blanks in steps 1-4 below will give a pretty accurate idea of when your first period will come. Of course, in order to do this, you need to have at least one older sister, and you'll need to know the age at which she began to menstruate. In fact, you'll need to know her age in years and months at the time of her first period. (If you have more than one older sister, it's your oldest sister's age you want.)

If your sister doesn't remember exactly, maybe someone else in the family or one of her friends can help you jog her memory. Anyway, do your best to figure out your sister's age at the time of her first menstrual period. Then, follow the directions in steps 1-4 below.

**1.** How many older brothers and sisters do you have? Write the the number on line 1.

1._____

**2.** Multiply the number on line 1 by 1¼ months and write the answer on line 2.

2._____mos

**3.** How old was your oldest sister when she started to menstruate? Write her age (in years and months) on line 3.

3.\_\_\_\_\_yrs\_\_\_\_mos

**4.** Subtract line 2 from line 3, and write the answer on line 4.

4.\_\_\_\_\_yrs\_\_\_\_mos

If your family follows this pattern, the answer on line 4 is the age at which you can expect your first menstrual period.

# Clue #2

Your stage of pubic hair growth and breast development can give you a clue as to when you'll have your first period. Which stage of pubic hair and breast development are you closest to right now? Before writing your answers in the space at the right, you might want to take another look at the stages shown on pages 34 and 38. (And, don't forget, it's possible to be in one stage of pubic hair growth and in another stage as far as breast development goes.)

Right now, I am in (or closest to) Stage _____ of pubic hair growth.

Right now, I am in (or closest to) Stage _____ of breast development.

The information in the chart below can give you some clue of when you'll start to menstruate.

This chart shows the percent of girls (the number of girls out of a group of 100 girls) who start to menstruate in each stage of breast development.

|  | Pubic Hair | Breast |
|---|---|---|
| Stage 1 | 1 | 0 |
| Stage 2 | 4 | 1 |
| Stage 3 | 19 | 26 |
| Stage 4 | 62 | 62 |
| Stage 5 | 14 | 11 |

★ **If you are in Stage 1 of breast and/or pubic hair development,** don't expect your period any time soon. It is highly unlikely that you'll start to menstruate before you develop more and progress to other stages. Only 1 girl in 100 will start to menstruate while she's still in Stage 1 of pubic hair growth, and no girls start to menstruate while they're in Stage 1 of breast development.

★ **If you are in Stage 2 of breast and/or pubic hair development,** you've got a way to go too. It is unlikely that you'll start to menstruate before you move to another stage. Only 1 out of 100 girls in Stage 2 of breast development and only 4 out of every 100 girls in Stage 2 of pubic hair growth will start to menstruate while they are in this stage.

★ **If you are in Stage 3 of breast and/or pubic hair growth,** there's a fair chance that you'll start to menstruate while you're still in this stage. But, it's more likely that you'll have to move to the next stage before you get your period. About 26 out of every 100 girls will start to menstruate while they are in Stage 3 of breast development, and about 19 out of every 100 girls will get their first period while they're in Stage 3 of pubic hair growth.

★ **If you're in Stage 4 of breast and/or pubic hair growth,** there is a very good chance you'll start to menstruate while you're in this stage. About 62 out of every 100 girls will start to menstruate while in Stage 4 of pubic hair and/or breast growth.

★ **If you're in Stage 5 of breast and/or pubic hair development** and you haven't started to menstruate yet, you can expect your period in the not-too-distant future. In fact, by the time they've entered Stage 5 of breast development, 86 out of every 100 girls have already begun to menstruate.

Likewise, 89 out of every 100 who enter Stage 5 of public hair growth have had their first periods.

• • • • • • • • • • • • • • • • • • • • • • • • • • • • • • • • • • •

## Summary: Clue #2

Most girls get their first periods while they're in Stage 4 of pubic hair and breast development. So if you're like most girls, that's when you'll get yours too.

Assuming that you will start to menstruate while in Breast Stage 4 and Pubic Hair Stage 4, you can figure out how many stages you have to go by subtracting your current Breast Stage and your current Pubic Hair Stage from Stage 4.

For example, Molly is in Breast Stage 2 and Pubic Hair Stage 3. Subtracting tells her that she has 2 more breast stages (the rest of Stage 2 and all of Stage 3) to go before she gets to Breast Stage 4 and that she has 1 more pubic hair stage (the rest of Stage 3) to go before she gets to Stage 4.

How many more stages do you have to go before you reach Breast Stage 4 and Pubic Hair Stage 4? Do your subtracting and then fill in the blanks below.

I have _____ breast stages to go before I reach Stage 4.

I have _____ pubic hair stages to go before I reach Stage 4.

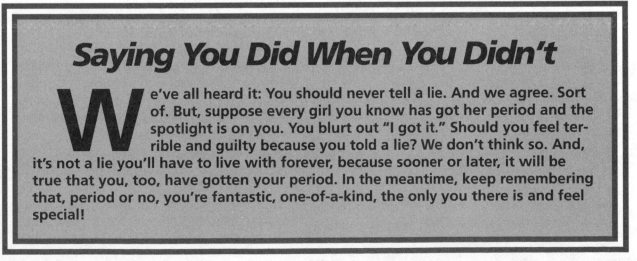

## Saying You Did When You Didn't

**W**e've all heard it: You should never tell a lie. And we agree. Sort of. But, suppose every girl you know has got her period and the spotlight is on you. You blurt out "I got it." Should you feel terrible and guilty because you told a lie? We don't think so. And, it's not a lie you'll have to live with forever, because sooner or later, it will be true that you, too, have gotten your period. In the meantime, keep remembering that, period or no, you're fantastic, one-of-a-kind, the only you there is and feel special!

# Clue #3

Clue #2 gave you a sense of how many stages you have left to go before you get your period. Now that you know *how far* you have left to go, the next question is *how long* will it take?

This third and final clue won't give you a definite answer to this question because each girl is different, and no one can say exactly how long it will take you to get through any given stage. But, Column II of the chart below will tell you the average amount of time that girls spend in each stage.

There's a wide variation in the amount of time normal girls take to go through these stages (and that's why we added Column III with a range of ages). For instance, if you read down Column I of the chart until you come to Pubic Hair Stage 3 and then read across the chart to Column II, you'll see that the average time for this stage is 12 months. But, in Column III, you'll see that most girls take between 2 months and 24 months to go through this stage. Of course, there are perfectly normal girls who will spend less than 2 months or more than 24 months in Pubic Hair Stage 3. The same is true for all the other ranges of time given in Column III.

## LENGTH OF TIME THAT IT TAKES TO GO THROUGH VARIOUS STAGES

| COLUMN I | COLUMN II | COLUMN III |
|---|---|---|
| Stage | The "Average" Time | Most Girls Will Take Between: |
| *Breast* | | |
| Stage 2 | About 11 months | About 2 to 18 months |
| Stage 3 | About 11 months | About 2 to 24 months |
| Stage 4 | About 20 months | About 8 to 24 months |
| *Pubic Hair* | | |
| Stage 2 | About 12 months | About 9 to 16 months |
| Stage 3 | About 12 months | About 2 to 24 months |
| Stage 4 | About 16 months | About 8 to 24 months |

# Using Clue #3

Figuring out how long it will take for you to get to Stage 4 requires a little bit of math, so here goes...

### Part I

**Step A)** Start by looking up your current pubic hair and breast development stages in Column I of the chart. Read across the chart to Column II and find the average amount of time girls spend in these stages. Remember, though, you've already done some of your time in these stages, so you'll need to move on to Step B.

**Step B)** Now subtract the time you've already spent in these stages. Estimate how long you've been in the breast stage you're currently in, and subtract that from the average amount of time girls spend in that stage (the number you found in step A above)*. For example, Li Ling estimates she's been in Stage 2 of breast development for about 3 months, and she knows this stage lasts an average of 11 months. So Li Ling subtracts 3 from 11 and finds that she has about 8 months to go before she makes it to the next stage. Now you try it for both breast and pubic hair development and write your answers below:

I probably have about____months to go before I reach the next Breast Stage.

I probably have about____months to go before I reach the next Pubic Hair Stage.

### Part II

**Are you currently in Stage 4 of pubic hair or breast development?** If you're currently in Stage 4 of pubic hair or breast development, you may start your period at any time now, but be sure to read the caution below.

**Are you currently in Stage 3 of pubic hair or breast development?** If you're in Breast Stage 3, write the number of months you have left in that stage in the circle inside the gray box below. If you're in Pubic Hair Stage 3, write the number of months you have left in that stage in the triangle inside the gray box below.

**Are you currently in Stage 2 of pubic hair or breast development?** If you're in Breast Stage 2, add 11 to the number of months you have left in this stage and write your answer in the circle inside the gray box below. If you're in Pubic Hair Stage 2, add 6 to the number of months you have left in this stage and write your answer in the triangle inside the grey box below.

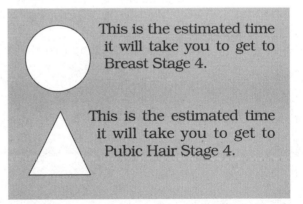

This is the estimated time it will take you to get to Breast Stage 4.

This is the estimated time it will take you to get to Pubic Hair Stage 4.

**REMEMBER**: These are just the average times, and each girl has her own special clock. Remember, too, that Breast Stage 4 lasts about 24 months and Pubic Hair Stage 4 lasts about 16 months. So, while you now have a better idea of when Stage 4 will hit, you still don't know when during Stage 4 your period may start.

---

* Your entries on pages 94–95 will help you make your estimate.

## You Got It!

Once you've gotten your first period, make it official by filling out the certificate below. Ask two very special people to witness your certification by signing their names in the spaces provided.

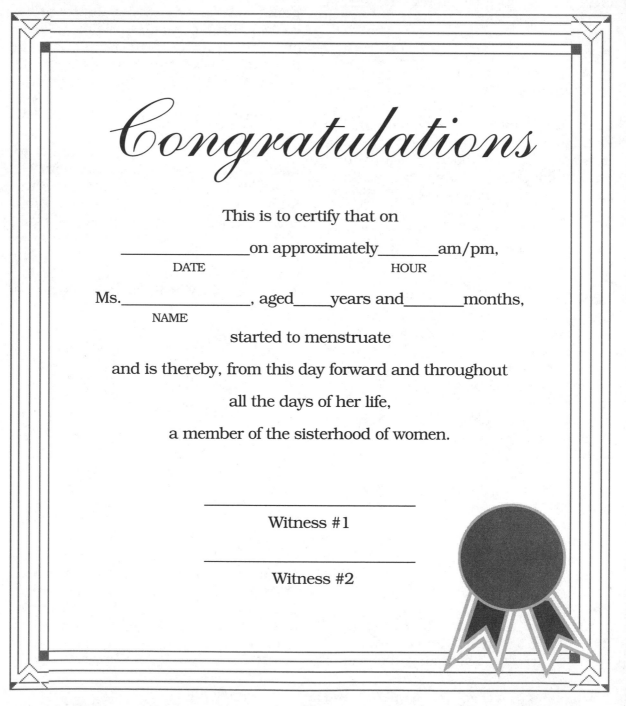

# Congratulations

This is to certify that on

_____on approximately_____am/pm,

DATE                                    HOUR

Ms._____, aged____years and_____months,

NAME

started to menstruate

and is thereby, from this day forward and throughout

all the days of her life,

a member of the sisterhood of women.

_____

Witness #1

_____

Witness #2

## Now, Write About It

You got it, now we want you to write about it. Use the space below to freewrite about the day (or night) you got your first period. (If you've forgotten how to freewrite, see page 9.)

Describe what happened when you got your first period. Tell where you were, who else was there, what time of day/night it was, how you knew you'd gotten it, what you did, who you told, how others reacted to your news, how you felt, or any other details about the big day.

On your mark, get set, freewrite!

Remember, when you are freewriting there's really only one rule: don't stop until you've filled the whole page.

## Menstrual Protection

There are two basic products on the market that will absorb the menstrual flow and protect your clothing from being stained: sanitary pads and tampons. Both forms of menstrual protection are made of soft fibers that absorb the flow. The difference is that pads are worn inside your underpants, while tampons are worn inside your vagina.

Which you use is a matter of personal choice. Some girls use one or the other exclusively. Others wear tampons during the day and use pads at night. There are also many girls who start out using pads and switch over to tampons when they're older, though it's okay to use tampons right from the beginning. It's really up to you.

There are 175 different styles and brands of tampons and pads on the market. There is also a new product, called inSync Miniforms, that gives protection for very light menstrual flow. The information and exercises in the next several pages will help you to choose the menstrual protection that works best for you.

## Sanitary Pads

The older style of pads that are worn with a sanitary pad belt or safety-pinned to your underpants are still on the market, but nowadays most women use the newer-style ones that are held in place by means of adhesive strips on the bottom of the napkin. To use the adhesive kind, you simply remove the glossy paper from

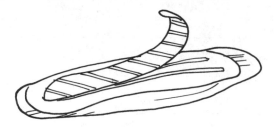

the adhesive and place the pad, sticky side down, on the inside of your underpants.

At first, wearing a pad can feel a little strange (like you're walking around with a rolled up beach towel between your legs). In reality, though, it's nowhere near that big, and no one can even tell that you're wearing one. Check yourself out in the mirror and you'll see—it really doesn't show.

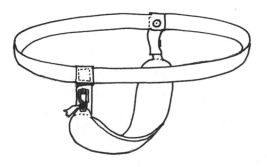

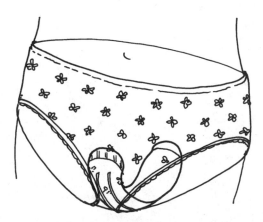

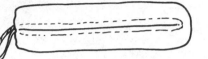
# Changing & Disposing Of Pads and Tampons

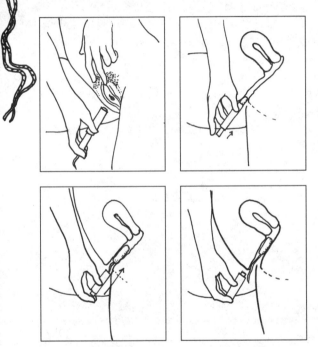

Tampons are small, tightly-rolled cylinders of cotton or other absorbent fibers that are inserted into the vagina to absorb the menstrual flow.

A tampon is inserted into the vagina by means of an applicator or simply by pushing it into place with your finger. Once in place, it fits snugly inside the vagina. It is held in place and prevented from slipping out by the tight muscles just inside the vaginal opening. The strings attached to the bottom of the tampon hang out of the vaginal opening. The tampon is removed by pulling gently on the string.

● A pad should be changed every four to six hours during the day so that it won't smell. Tampons should always be changed every four to eight hours. At night consider using a pad rather than a tampon.

● Even if you have a very light flow and don't have to worry about soaking through, you should change pads and tampons frequently. Menstrual blood itself is perfectly clean and odorless, but once outside the uterus, it comes in contact with the germs. Though these germs aren't necessarily harmful, they grow very rapidly in blood and can cause an unpleasant odor. By changing your pad frequently, you won't give the germs and odor a chance to develop.

● Changing tampons frequently is especially important, because it reduces the risk of an infection known as toxic shock syndrome that tampon users can develop (see page 103).

● When you change pads, wrap the soiled one in toilet paper. (This will help cut down on odor developing in the soiled napkin.) Deposit the wrapped pad in the trash or in the container for used napkins.

● Never flush pads down the toilet; they can clog the plumbing.

● It's OK to flush the tampon itself down the toilet (unless you have really ancient plumbing). But don't flush the tampon applicators or packaging as they, too, can clog the pipes.

# Inserting A Tampon For The Very First Time

The instruction sheets that come inside the box make inserting a tampon sound about as easy as building a space shuttle. But you don't need to be a rocket scientist to use a tampon. Of course, the first time can be a little confusing and *a lot* frustrating. But between the instructions in the box and these tips, you'll do just fine!

## Tips For First-Time Users

Use the smallest size: Junior absorbency tampons are the thinnest and easiest to insert.

Know where you're going: Get a mirror and look at your vaginal opening. (There's a helpful illustration on page 64.) Putting your finger inside your vagina and tightening your muscles will show you how strong these muscles are. Even when you're completely relaxed, these muscles are tight enough to prevent the tampon from slipping out. When you insert a tampon, push it far enough up into the vagina so it's past those muscles. Otherwise, the tampon will be caught in these muscles and you'll feel rather uncomfortable.

Insert the tampon at an angle: Your vagina doesn't go straight up and down; it angles toward your lower back (see the illustration on page 72). Aiming the tampon straight up isn't going to work. Instead, point it toward the small of your back (the lower curving part of your back).

Relax: If you're tense, your vaginal muscles tighten up, which makes insertion difficult, if not impossible. Take a few slow, deep breaths, relaxing as you breathe out.

Use lubrication: If your vagina is dry, use saliva or some K-Y jelly (not vaseline, scented perfumes, or lotions). A little lubrication on the tip of the tampon really helps.

Removal: This is easy — simply pull the string. Sometimes, the string works its way up into the vagina, in which case, just reach up into your vagina and pull the tampon out. (The tampon will be easier to reach if you bear down, as if you were making a bowel movement.)

"Forgotten tampons": Tampons are so comfortable, you may forget you have one in. If you've forgotten to remove a tampon, just take it out as soon as you remember. There may be an unpleasant odor, but this should clear up on its own within (at most) few days.

Hotline: Tambrands, the makers of Tampax® tampons, has a hotline number that tampax users can call for answers to questions about tampons or menstruation. Just call 1-800-523-0014 between 8:00 am and 5:00 pm, Eastern Time, Monday through Friday.

## Toxic Shock Syndrome (TSS): Are Tampons Safe?

TSS is short for toxic shock syndrome, which is a rare, but very serious—sometimes deadly—infection that has been associated with the use of tampons. Although TSS has affected people of all ages and both sexes, the majority of cases have occurred during the menstrual period in young women who were using tampons at the time the infection developed.

It's not that tampons are infected or carry germs. Tampons themselves don't actually cause TSS. The infection is caused by a very common bacteria that are normal inhabitants of many people's bodies. These bacteria live on the surface of the skin and in the various cavities of the body, including the vagina. Normally, though, they don't cause problems. However, in a small number of women, these bacteria do cause TSS, and in most cases TSS has occurred in women using highly absorbent tampons.

Why? Doctors aren't entirely sure. But, blood is a rich breeding ground for bacteria. Leaving a tampon in too long allows the bacteria to multiply to the point where an infection occurs. Women who use the super absorbent kind of tampon are especially prone because they tend to change their tampons less often (which is a big no-no).

It's unclear why an infection in the vagina can suddenly escalate into a life-threatening condition affecting the whole body. Some experts think that tiny scratches in the walls of the vagina, caused by fingernails or the tip of a plastic tampon applicator, allow the bacteria to get into the bloodstream so that the infection affects the whole body. Still other experts think that the problem lies with certain types of synthetic fibers used in some tampons, which may increase the bacteria's ability to produce the toxins which cause TSS. Whatever the cause, TSS is very rare. Typically, TSS begins with sudden high fever, muscle aches, diarrhea, vomiting, inflamed eyes, and a sunburn-like rash

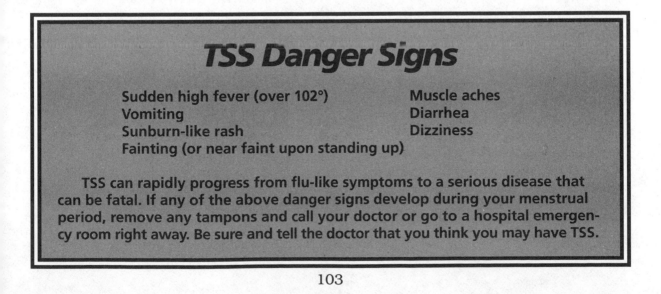

## TSS Danger Signs

Sudden high fever (over 102°)  Muscle aches
Vomiting  Diarrhea
Sunburn-like rash  Dizziness
Fainting (or near faint upon standing up)

TSS can rapidly progress from flu-like symptoms to a serious disease that can be fatal. If any of the above danger signs develop during your menstrual period, remove any tampons and call your doctor or go to a hospital emergency room right away. Be sure and tell the doctor that you think you may have TSS.

which may surface after a few days. In very severe cases there may be kidney, heart, liver, and blood-clotting problems as well as low blood-pressure. Usually people recover from TSS.

# Should You Use Tampons?

The decision of whether or not to use tampons is a personal one. You can practically eliminate your chances of getting TSS by using sanitary napkins instead of tampons. Even if you do use tampons, though, your risk of getting TSS is very low. You can reduce this risk even further by taking the following precautions:

● Use tampons that are not highly absorbent (those with a rating of regular or junior—see page 109), and change them at least once every four to eight hours, even when your flow is light.

● Wear a pad to bed at night (since you won't be awake to change a tampon).

● Wash your hands before inserting a tampon, and insert the tampon carefully to avoid carrying bacteria from your skin or rectum into your vagina.

● If you use the type of tampon that doesn't have an applicator (see page 108), make sure your nails are short and smooth, without snags, and be careful not to tear or scratch the opening or walls of your vagina while inserting the tampon.

● If you use the type of tampon that comes inside a plastic applicator (see page 108), be careful not to tear or scratch the opening or walls of your vagina while inserting the tampon.

## Marvelous Menstruating Moments...

*When you first realize your blood has come, smile; an honest smile, for you are about to have an intense union with your magic. This is a private time, a special time, for thinking and dreaming. Change your bedsheet to the ones that are your favorite. Sleep with a laurel leaf under your head. Take baths with wild hyssop, white water lilies. Listen for the voices of your visions; they are nearby. Let annoying people, draining worries, fall away as your body lets what she doesn't need go from her. Remember that you are a river; your banks are red honey where the Moon wanders.*

*From the novel* Sassafrass Cypress & Indigo *by Ntozake Shange*

# Test Your
# I.Q.
## with This
# P.Q.
## (Puberty Quiz)

| True | False | |
|------|-------|---|
| ____ | ____ | **1.** A tampon can "go up inside" and get lost inside your body. |
| ____ | ____ | **2.** You can use a tampon during your first period. |
| ____ | ____ | **3.** Because there are other body openings in the area, a girl can easily insert a tampon in the wrong place. |
| ____ | ____ | **4.** You can go swimming or participate in any other sports when you have your period. |
| ____ | ____ | **5.** Using a tampon is painful. |
| ____ | ____ | **6.** You should remove your tampon before urinating (going to the bathroom). |
| ____ | ____ | **7.** You can't feel a tampon that has been inserted properly. |
| ____ | ____ | **8.** You should change your tampons every three or four hours. |
| ____ | ____ | **9.** Inserting a tampon tears or "breaks" a girl's hymen. |
| ____ | ____ | **10.** If a tampon is inserted correctly, it will not leak. |

# Answers

**1. False.** A tampon can't "go up inside" your body or get lost inside you. Except when it expands for childbirth, the opening to the cervical canal (see p.71) is too small for a tampon to pass through. Occasionally the tampon removal string will work its way into your vagina. Then you have to feel inside your vagina for the string in order to remove the tampon. Bearing down as if you were making a bowel movement will help bring the string within reach.

**2. True.** Anyone can use a tampon, even if it's your first period.

**3. False.** Though we won't say it's medically impossible to accidently insert a tampon into the anus or urinary opening, it certainly wouldn't be an easy mistake to make. These other openings, particularly the urinary opening are nowhere near as elastic as the vaginal opening, so attempting to insert a tampon would cause so much discomfort that most people would stop trying long before they could actually succeed in insertion.

**4. True.** You can go swimming while you're having a period, but it's best to use a tampon. Swimming with a napkin could get awfully soggy!

**5. False.** But it can be a little difficult to insert a tampon the first time, especially if you're nervous. If you have trouble, you might try using a little K-Y jelly on the applicator or gently stretching your vaginal opening with your finger from time to time, and eventually you should be able to insert the tampon easily.

**6. False.** Your body has a separate hole from which you urinate, and there is no need to remove or replace a tampon when you urinate.

**7. True.** Once a tampon is properly in place, you can't feel it. If you can feel it, it isn't in far enough.

**8. True.** It's possible to get a very serious infection known as Toxic Shock Syndrome (see page 103) from using tampons. However, it is very rare, and you can help prevent it by changing your tampon every three or four hours and using pads at night.

**9. False.** A girl's hymen has one or more holes in it and is very stretchy, so a tampon can be placed in your vagina without injuring your hymen.

**10. False.** Tampons can leak even if you change them often enough and insert them properly (see page 101).

# *A Buyers Guide:* SANITARY NAPKINS

Super maxi plus...thin maxi pads...thin super maxi pads...ultra slim super thin extra protection maxi pads—this guide will help you make sense of the confusing variety of products on the market. Pads range in thickness from the very thin and least absorbent panty liners to the thickest and most absorbent super maxi pads.

**PANTY LINERS:** (Also called panty shields or protectors.) These might be useful as a "back-up," in case your tampon leaks; otherwise, they're too thin and absorb too little to be of any real use.

**MINI PADS:** Thicker than panty liners, but still small and slim. They're good for days when your menstrual flow is light.

**SLENDER OR JUNIOR PADS:** Shorter and slimmer maxi pads , designed especially for teens.

**THIN MAXI PADS:** Thicker than mini pads, but thinner than regular maxi pads, for medium to heavy flow.

**REGULAR MAXI PADS:** (or just plain "maxi" pads) These are somewhat thicker (in between the thin and super maxi pads), for days when flow is heavier.

**SUPER MAXI PADS:** Thickest, most absorbent pads—"extra" protection at night or if your flow is especially heavy. Some companies also make a "thin super maxi pad" that is more absorbent than a regular maxi pad, but not as bulky as a super maxi.

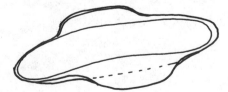

The various brands on the market aren't dramatically different from one another, except that some have "wings" that wrap around the sides of your panties and supposedly help prevent "leaking."

# A Buyer's Guide: TAMPONS

You have four styles of tampons to choose from, depending on which method of insertion you prefer.

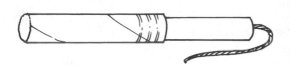

**CARDBOARD TUBE APPLICATOR:** The tampon comes packed in the upper tube of a two-part cardboard applicator. The tip of the upper tube is inserted into the vagina. Pressing on the lower tube then pushes the tampon out of the applicator and into the vagina.

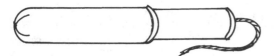

**PLASTIC APPLICATOR:** This type of tampon comes packed inside a plastic applicator that basically works the same way as the cardboard applicator described above.

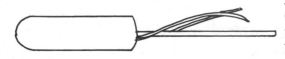

**STICK APPLICATOR:** This type of tampon doesn't come inside an applicator. Instead, there is a detachable stick in the center of the base of the tampon, which is used to push the tampon into the vagina and is then detached with a slight tug.

**NO APPLICATOR:** This type of tampon doesn't have an applicator. You simply use your finger to push the tampon into the vagina.

# Choosing the Right Absorbency

Y ou want to choose tampon absorbent enough that you don't have to run to the bathroom every ten minutes to change it. But, because the risk of getting toxic shock syndrome (see page 103) appears to be greater with the more highly absorbent tampons, medical experts advise using the least absorbent tampon that will meet your protection needs. A good rule of thumb is: If you have to change your tampon more than every couple of hours, try a higher absorbency tampon for the days of heavy flow. But if your vagina feels dry or the tampon "sticks" when it's being removed, you need a lower absorbency tampon, at least on light days.

## What They Mean

You also have a choice of four sizes, or absorbencies. Tampons are rated on a standard scale, according to how much fluid they can absorb.

Junior absorbency tampons, the least absorbent tampons, are also the slimmest and the easiest to insert. Super plus, the most absorbent, are the thickest and absorb heavy flow most effectively.

# "Starter" Kits

Trying out a variety of menstrual products to see which you like best is a great idea. But, buying a box of all the different brands could cost you a small fortune. Luckily, some companies offer free or low cost "starter kits" that contain samples of the pads and/or tampons the company makes.

✿ **inSync Miniforms:** inSync offers free samples to new users. Call their 24-hour, toll-free number: 888-846-7962.

✿ **Kotex pads, New Freedom pads, Lightdays pantiliners, and Security tampons:** You must contact the company to request an order form. Go to http://www.kimberly-clark.com/ask/response/cgi or write to Education Programs, 8003 Old York Road, Elkins, PA 19117-1410.

✿ **Playtex Slimfit, SilkGlide, and Gentle Guide tampons:** Go to http://www.playtextampons.com or write to Consumer Affairs Department, Playtex Products, Inc., PO Box 728, Paramus, NJ 07652.

✿ **Stayfree pads, Carefree pantiliners pads, o.b. tampons:** Go to http://www.cyclesofwellness.com

✿ **Tampax tampons:** Go to http://www.beinggirl.com

✿ **Always pads:** Go to http://www.always.com or http://www.always.com/growing/

## Ask a Woman Who Knows

Your mom or another adult woman you trust will have some helpful advice about menstrual products. Ask a woman who knows the following questions.

1. Do you use napkins or tampons or both? Why have you chosen this type of menstrual product?_____

_____

_____

2. Have you tried a lot of different brands? Do you have a favorite? If so, why do you like this particular product? _____

_____

3. What did you use when you were my age?_____

4. What would you recommend I use?_____

_____

## FLY ME TO THE MOON

There are more than 70 million menstruating women in the U.S. They spend well over one billion dollars to purchase around 12 billion sanitary pads each year. Laid end to end this number of pads would equal roughly 1.6 million miles–enough for three round trips to the moon. In addition, American women spend another $700 million, or so, to purchase approximately 6 billion tampons.

# What Would You Do?

**1.** Justine started her period about six months ago. Since then her mother has been buying her pads every month. That was fine with Justine in the winter and spring, but now it's summertime. Justine is swimming every day, and she hopes to swim for her team in the big meet at the end of the summer. She wants to wear tampons so she won't miss practice when she's on her period. When she asks if she could start using tampons, her mother says she is "too young." When she later asks again, her mom still says no.

**What could Justine do?**

_____

_____

_____

**2.** Jane has to go to the store to buy herself tampons. She's never done this alone before, so she's very nervous. When she gets in line she realizes that the box boy is a real cute guy she knows from school. Jane is so embarrassed she doesn't know what to do.

**Do you have any suggestions for Jane?**

_____

_____

_____

_____

**3.** Cecily changes napkins frequently, and she always knows her period has come long before any blood could soak through and show on her clothes. So, all those stories of girls unknowingly walking around with menstrual blood on their clothes don't worry Cecily. After all, how many girls with blood-stained clothes has she ever seen?—None! Then one day, Cecily is standing in the school cafeteria lunch line, when her best friend whispers in her ear, "There's blood on the back of your skirt."

**What can Cecily do?**

_____

_____

_____

**4.** Anna is twelve and a half years old. She hasn't gotten her period yet, but she knows she could get it at any time. She's excited about it. One thing really bothers her though—"What will I do if I get it at school?"

**Do you have any advice for Anna?**

_____

_____

_____

Now, turn the page and compare your advice to the advice others have given.

## 1. Justine could:

✔ Talk to her mom and try and find out why she doesn't want her to use tampons.

✔ Get a copy of a booklet put out by a tampon manufacturer (see Starter Kits, page 109) and show it to her mother. (Her mom may not be aware that it's safe and perfectly fine for a girl just her age to use tampons.)

✔ Write her mom a letter explaining why she wants to use tampons and why she feels it's safe. That way, her mom may be more likely to take her request seriously.

## 2. Jane could:

✔ Switch to another checkout line or try another store. (It's okay to do that if the situation is too uncomfortable!)

✔ Pretend she's buying them for her mother and just act like it's no big deal.

✔ Just do it. So what if he thinks you menstruate—you do! Besides, checkout clerks see tampons and pads going into bags all day long. They hardly even notice.

## 3. Cecily could:

✔ Shift her skirt around so the spot is in a place she can cover with her purse, her books or her hand until she can get to the girls room and wash her skirt.

✔ Quickly sit at the nearest table. Have her friend get her lunch and stay there until everyone is gone. Then go to the nurse's or school office for help.

✔ Have her friend walk in back of her (without being real obvious), go to the Home Ec room and ask the teacher for help cleaning the skirt (and for a late pass, if she'll need it for her next class).

## 4. Anna could:

✔ Ask to be excused from class and go to the girls room and buy a pad or tampon from the machine.

✔ Go to the nurse's office (she's bound to have one).

✔ Keep a pad or tampon in your purse so you'll be ready. (Purse size carrying kits are available for both pads and tampons.)

✔ Go to the school office and ask the secretary for a pad or tampon.

✔ Ask a friend or a nice teacher for one.

✔ Keep a pad or tampon in your locker.

✔ Make a temporary pad out of toilet paper and then get a real pad as soon as you can.

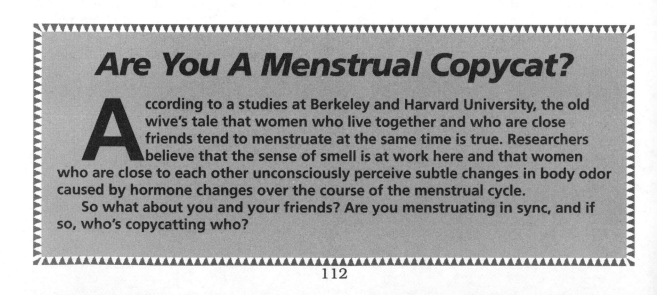

# Are You A Menstrual Copycat?

**A**ccording to a studies at Berkeley and Harvard University, the old wive's tale that women who live together and who are close friends tend to menstruate at the same time is true. Researchers believe that the sense of smell is at work here and that women who are close to each other unconsciously perceive subtle changes in body odor caused by hormone changes over the course of the menstrual cycle.

So what about you and your friends? Are you menstruating in sync, and if so, who's copycatting who?

# *Do You Ever Have Cramps?*

**YES**

Do your cramps occur in 7-10 days before your period?

**YES**

You may have PMS. See p. 114.

**NO**

**NO**

You're lucky! But if your luck changes be sure to come back here!

---

## RATE YOUR CRAMPS                    *write answers here*

Do you get cramps with your period?

| | |
|---|---|
| Only once in a while | Score 0 |
| Sometimes | Score 1 |
| Usually/always | Score 2 |

Do you have to stay in bed or miss school?

| | |
|---|---|
| Never | Score 0 |
| Sometimes | Score 1 |
| Usually/always | Score 2 |

Do they last more than 24 hours?

| | |
|---|---|
| Never | Score 0 |
| Only once in a while | Score 1 |
| Usually/always | Score 2 |

Now, add up your total score and enter it here:_____

---

Is your score more than 4?

**YES**

**NO**

---

**See your doctor.**

Bad cramps could be a sign of some other medical problem that deserves attention. Also, your doctor can prescribe pain medicine and antiprostaglandins, which work against prostaglandins, a hormone that can cause the uterus to contract sharply during menstruation, producing cramps.

**Self-help remedies:**
- ◯ A heating pad or hot water bottle on your lower abdomen may feel good.
- ◯ Some women find that masturbation is helpful.
- ◯ Exercises (see page 115) often help to relieve crampy feeling.
- ◯ Avoid fatty, salty foods.

**Non-prescription drugs:**
- ◯ Non-aspirin pain relievers
- ◯ Other pain relievers made especially for menstrual cramps. Products containing ibuprofen are good.

113

# Quick Check

1) Are your breasts swollen and tender before your period? ❏ Yes ❏ No

2) Do you develop cravings for chocolate or other sweets (cake, ice cream, and candy) just before your period? ❏ Yes ❏ No

3) Do you have bloating and/or a temporary gain of a few pounds each month? ❏ Yes ❏ No

4) Are you sometimes constipated before your period, but then have diarrhea when you begin to menstruate? ❏ Yes ❏ No

5) Do you have trouble getting a good night's sleep in the week before your period comes? ❏ Yes ❏ No

6) Are you absentminded, confused, forgetful, or disorganized in the days before your period starts? ❏ Yes ❏ No

7) Do you feel out of control for no obvious reason at any time during the two weeks before your period? ❏ Yes ❏ No

8) Do you have cramps that begin sometime in the two weeks prior to your period and that end once the menstrual flow begins? ❏ Yes ❏ No

**Scoring:** The more "yes" answers you gave, the more likely it is that you have PMS.

What's PMS?—Read the box below and you'll find out.

## PMS: Premenstrual Syndrome

Premenstrual Syndrome is a medical condition that affects different women in different ways and can produce a wide variety of physical and psychological symptoms. The symptoms, which may be mild, moderate, or quite severe, begin in the two weeks prior to—and are usually relieved by—menstruation. Common physical symptoms include bloating, weight gain, breast pain, backache, cramps, pimples, and a craving for sweets. Feelings of tension, depression, and sleep problems are some of the common psychological symptoms.

The condition is more common in older women, but can affect girls just starting to menstruate too. The causes are not well understood, but it is believed that hormones, body chemistry, and nutrition may play a role. Treatment for the condition includes: eating balanced meals with foods rich in vitamin B6, and magnesium (green vegetables, whole grains, nuts, and seeds). Some doctors use hormones to treat PMS. But others are not sure that hormone treatments really work.

# Exercises For Cramps

**1.** Stand with your back against the wall, with your shoulders, heels, head, and as much of your body touching the wall as possible. Keep your chin level, but pretend there's a string attached to the top of your head that is pulling you up-ward, stretching you up as tall as possible.

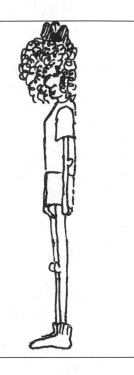

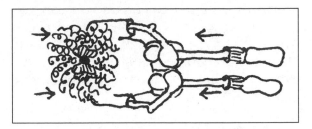

**3.** Lie on your side, bring your knees up to your chest, tuck your head under, and try to touch your chin to your knees.

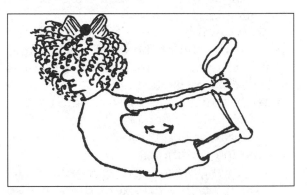

**2.** Lie flat on the floor, face down, palms on the floor beside your shoulders. Slowly push your palms down on the floor, and raise your head and shoulders off the floor until your arms are outstretched and your back is arched. Repeat several times.

**4.** Lie flat on the floor, face down. Stretch your arms behind you, grab your ankles, bending your knees and bringing your feet up to meet your hands. Gently rock back and forth in this position.

# Your Menstrual Calendar

On the facing page, there's a year's worth of undated calendars you can use to keep track of your menstrual cycle. We've left off the names of the months and days so you can begin using the calendars when you have your first (or your next) period.

## Using the Calendars

When you get your period:

✿ Circle the date that it starts on the first calendar.

✿ Write the name of the month in the space at the top of the first calendar and fill in the names of the following months on the remaining calendars.

✿ If a month has less than 31 days, cross out the extra days.

✿ Draw a line through each day that your period continues.

✿ Each time you get your period, circle the date it starts and draw a line through each day that the bleeding continues.

For example, if your period began June 6th and continued until the 12th, your first month's calendar would look like this:

| June | | | 1 | 2 | 3 |
|---|---|---|---|---|---|
| 4 | 5 | ⑥ | 7̸ | 8̸ | 9̸ | 1̸0̸ |
| 1̸1̸ | 1̸2̸ | 13 | 14 | 15 | 16 | 17 |
| 18 | 19 | 20 | 21 | 22 | 23 | 24 |
| 25 | 26 | 27 | 28 | 29 | 30 | 3̸1̸ |

*Note that the 31st day is crossed off because June has only 30 days.*

## Determining the Length of Your Cycle

As you learned in Part 5, the menstrual cycle includes the entire cycle of ovulation and menstruation and runs from the first day of bleeding of one menstrual period to the first day of bleeding of the next cycle. The length of the cycle may vary from one cycle to the next, especially in the first few years of menstruating. In grown women, the cycle is usually between 21 to 36 days long, with 28 days being the average. It may take as long as three years before a girl develops a regular pattern of menstruating. Once young women do establish a pattern, their normal cycle length ranges from 20 to 45 days.

To determine the length of a menstrual cycle on your calendars, count the number of days from one circled day to the next. Don't include the second circled day in your count.

## How Long Was Your Cycle?

Suppose that, as in the example at the left, you got your period on June 6th. Then, as indicated on the calendar below, your period began on July 13th. How long was your menstrual cycle?

| July | | | 1 | 2 | 3 |
|---|---|---|---|---|---|
| 4 | 5 | 6 | 7 | 8 | 9 | 10 |
| 11 | 12 | ⑬ | 1̸4̸ | 1̸5̸ | 1̸6̸ | 1̸7̸ |
| 1̸8̸ | 19 | 20 | 21 | 22 | 23 | 24 |
| 25 | 26 | 27 | 28 | 29 | 30 | 31 |

Answer: The cycle was 38 days long.

|  |  |  | 1 | 2 | 3 |
|---|---|---|---|---|---|
| 4 | 5 | 6 | 7 | 8 | 9 | 10 |
| 11 | 12 | 13 | 14 | 15 | 16 | 17 |
| 18 | 19 | 20 | 21 | 22 | 23 | 24 |
| 25 | 26 | 27 | 28 | 29 | 30 | 31 |

|  |  |  | 1 | 2 | 3 |
|---|---|---|---|---|---|
| 4 | 5 | 6 | 7 | 8 | 9 | 10 |
| 11 | 12 | 13 | 14 | 15 | 16 | 17 |
| 18 | 19 | 20 | 21 | 22 | 23 | 24 |
| 25 | 26 | 27 | 28 | 29 | 30 | 31 |

|  |  |  | 1 | 2 | 3 |
|---|---|---|---|---|---|
| 4 | 5 | 6 | 7 | 8 | 9 | 10 |
| 11 | 12 | 13 | 14 | 15 | 16 | 17 |
| 18 | 19 | 20 | 21 | 22 | 23 | 24 |
| 25 | 26 | 27 | 28 | 29 | 30 | 31 |

|  |  |  | 1 | 2 | 3 |
|---|---|---|---|---|---|
| 4 | 5 | 6 | 7 | 8 | 9 | 10 |
| 11 | 12 | 13 | 14 | 15 | 16 | 17 |
| 18 | 19 | 20 | 21 | 22 | 23 | 24 |
| 25 | 26 | 27 | 28 | 29 | 30 | 31 |

|  |  |  | 1 | 2 | 3 |
|---|---|---|---|---|---|
| 4 | 5 | 6 | 7 | 8 | 9 | 10 |
| 11 | 12 | 13 | 14 | 15 | 16 | 17 |
| 18 | 19 | 20 | 21 | 22 | 23 | 24 |
| 25 | 26 | 27 | 28 | 29 | 30 | 31 |

|  |  |  | 1 | 2 | 3 |
|---|---|---|---|---|---|
| 4 | 5 | 6 | 7 | 8 | 9 | 10 |
| 11 | 12 | 13 | 14 | 15 | 16 | 17 |
| 18 | 19 | 20 | 21 | 22 | 23 | 24 |
| 25 | 26 | 27 | 28 | 29 | 30 | 31 |

|  |  |  | 1 | 2 | 3 |
|---|---|---|---|---|---|
| 4 | 5 | 6 | 7 | 8 | 9 | 10 |
| 11 | 12 | 13 | 14 | 15 | 16 | 17 |
| 18 | 19 | 20 | 21 | 22 | 23 | 24 |
| 25 | 26 | 27 | 28 | 29 | 30 | 31 |

|  |  |  | 1 | 2 | 3 |
|---|---|---|---|---|---|
| 4 | 5 | 6 | 7 | 8 | 9 | 10 |
| 11 | 12 | 13 | 14 | 15 | 16 | 17 |
| 18 | 19 | 20 | 21 | 22 | 23 | 24 |
| 25 | 26 | 27 | 28 | 29 | 30 | 31 |

|  |  |  | 1 | 2 | 3 |
|---|---|---|---|---|---|
| 4 | 5 | 6 | 7 | 8 | 9 | 10 |
| 11 | 12 | 13 | 14 | 15 | 16 | 17 |
| 18 | 19 | 20 | 21 | 22 | 23 | 24 |
| 25 | 26 | 27 | 28 | 29 | 30 | 31 |

|  |  |  | 1 | 2 | 3 |
|---|---|---|---|---|---|
| 4 | 5 | 6 | 7 | 8 | 9 | 10 |
| 11 | 12 | 13 | 14 | 15 | 16 | 17 |
| 18 | 19 | 20 | 21 | 22 | 23 | 24 |
| 25 | 26 | 27 | 28 | 29 | 30 | 31 |

|  |  |  | 1 | 2 | 3 |
|---|---|---|---|---|---|
| 4 | 5 | 6 | 7 | 8 | 9 | 10 |
| 11 | 12 | 13 | 14 | 15 | 16 | 17 |
| 18 | 19 | 20 | 21 | 22 | 23 | 24 |
| 25 | 26 | 27 | 28 | 29 | 30 | 31 |

|  |  |  | 1 | 2 | 3 |
|---|---|---|---|---|---|
| 4 | 5 | 6 | 7 | 8 | 9 | 10 |
| 11 | 12 | 13 | 14 | 15 | 16 | 17 |
| 18 | 19 | 20 | 21 | 22 | 23 | 24 |
| 25 | 26 | 27 | 28 | 29 | 30 | 31 |

# Further Reading

Bell, Ruth. **Changing Bodies, Changing Lives: A Book for Teens on Sex and Relationships** revised edition (New York: Random House, 1998).

A fine book, representing many points of view through quotes from teenagers themselves. The section on teenage pregnancy is especially good, and the one on mental health, depression, and suicide is outstanding. The book is geared toward the fifteen- to nineteen-year-old age group, but it could be valuable for younger and older people as well.

Calderone, Mary S., M.D. and Johnson, Eric W. **The Family Book About Sexuality** (New York: HarperCollins, 1990).

Designed for the whole family, this book talks about how sexuality begins when we are only tiny babies, and how it develops through puberty and adulthood, and even into old age.

Madaras, Lynda and Area. **My Feelings, My Self: A Growing-Up Guide for Girls** (New York: Newmarket Press, 2000).

For pre-teens and teens, a workbook/journal to help girls explore their relationships with parents and friends. It includes quizzes, exercises, and space to record personal experiences.

Madaras, Lynda with Area. **The "What's Happening to My Body?" Book for Boys** (New York: Newmarket Press, 2000)

This is a book that I wrote for boys about puberty. Needless to say, we think it's a pretty good one. Although it was written for boys, many girls and parents have read it and told us they learned a lot from it.

Madaras, Lynda with Area. **The "What's Happening to My Body?" Book for Girls** (New York: Newmarket Press, 2000)

This is the companion book to My Body, My Self in which we explain the body changes that take place in a girl's body during puberty. It has a lot more detailed information than we had room for in this book. If you have unanswered questions, we'd be willing to bet you'll find the answers here.

Planned Parenthood. **Kids Need to Know.**

This is an information kit for parents and teens that includes booklets and pamphlets on topics such as sexuality and birth control. The kit is available from the Information and Education Department, Planned Parenthood, 1316 Third Street Promenade, Suite B5, Santa Monica, California 90401.

# LYNDA MADARAS BOOKS FOR PRE-TEENS AND TEENS (AND THEIR FAMILIES, FRIENDS, AND TEACHERS)

Order from your local bookstore or write or call:
Newmarket Press, 18 East 48th Street, New York, NY 10017;
(212) 832-3575 or (800) 669-3903; Fax (212) 832-3629;
E-mail sales@newmarketpress.com

Please send me the following books by Lynda Madaras:

THE "WHAT'S HAPPENING TO MY BODY?" BOOK FOR GIRLS
_____ copies at $22.95 each (gift hardcover)
_____ copies at $12.95 each (trade paperback)

THE "WHAT'S HAPPENING TO MY BODY?" BOOK FOR BOYS
_____ copies at $22.95 each (gift hardcover)
_____ copies at $12.95 each (trade paperback)

MY BODY, MY SELF FOR GIRLS
_____ copies at $12.95 each (trade paperback)

MY BODY, MY SELF FOR BOYS
_____ copies at $12.95 each (trade paperback)

MY FEELINGS, MY SELF (A Growing-Up Guide For Girls}
_____ copies at $12.95 each (trade paperback)

For postage and handling, add $3.00 for the first book, plus $1.00 for each additional book. Please allow 4-6 weeks for delivery. Prices and availability subject to change.

I enclose a check or money order, payable to Newmarket Press, in the

amount of $_____.

(NY residents please add sales tax.)

Name _____

Address _____

City/State/Zip _____

Special discounts are available for orders of five or more copies.
For information, contact Newmarket Press, Special Sales Dept.,
18 East 48th Street, New York, NY 10017;
(212) 832-3575 or (800) 669-3903; Fax (212) 832-3629 ;
E-mail sales@newmarketpress.com